BIKE HIKING

STEVE SHERMAN, a graduate of Loyola University of Los Angeles, is the author of numerous articles for a wide variety of trade journals and magazines and of a book on library promotion. An experienced traveler by bike, foot, and car, Mr. Sherman currently lives in New Hampshire.

STEVE SHERMAN

BIKE
HIKING

DOLPHIN BOOKS
DOUBLEDAY & COMPANY, INC.
GARDEN CITY, NEW YORK

ISBN: 0-385-01805-3
Library of Congress Catalog Card Number 73–11731
Copyright © 1974 by Steve Sherman
Printed in the United States of America

CONTENTS

BIKE HIKING

1

TO BIKE OR NOT TO BIKE

The sky is high and blue and the open road slants down the earth. The wind is at your back. The spokes of your shiny two-wheeler zing through the atmosphere as if you were sailing six feet off the ground. You're pedaling to beat the band. For all you know it could be destination moon.

You crouch to reduce wind resistance, to keep the center of gravity low. You're on a machine, not in one. You're the power and the glory. The new rhythm swashes through your body. It's in your blowing hair and churning bones. It's in your pumping insides. Simplicity. Fullness. Exhilaration. It just feels *good*.

You know what you're doing. You're riding the world. You're riding a bike.

MILLIONS DO

More than eighty million young, old, and middle-aged Americans ride bicycles today. The Bicycle Institute of America estimates that eleven and a half million bicycles were sold in 1972, more than two and a half million over the previous year. Americans are discovering the new world.

No longer is bike riding left to children. The percentage of adults buying bicycles for themselves instead of their sons and daughters jumped from 12 per cent in 1969 to 50 per cent in 1972. Many of these riders cycle around the block, some around the town, still others around the state. Some ride for better blood circulation, others for losing weight, but undoubtedly nearly 100 per cent of them ride first of all because it's simply fun. Think about it. When was the last time you met a grouchy bike rider?

THE IDEAL COMPROMISE

A bike is an ideal compromise between walking and a car. A bike triples the speed of walking yet doesn't zoom over the landscape, so that what is passed isn't passed unseen. Besides that, a bike rider is not encapsuled in an elegant tank like an automobile driver is, nor does a bike rider transform himself from a rational human being into one of the merciless combatants that kills 56,000 people on the highways in the United States each year. A bicycle somehow engenders a more tolerant, relaxed outlook on fellow men and women. Bike riders don't share the death-dealing aggression that comes with car driving. Moreover, bicyclists don't claim an inflated territory around their machines as do car drivers around their dicta from Detroit. As one and all know, nobody but nobody cuts off another freeway driver with impunity.

Speed may be one softening factor. While Jose Meiffret set the world speed record for bicycles when he rode 127.342 miles per hour in 1962, most bike riders are content with, and indeed capable of, between ten and twenty miles per hour. As a result, a refreshing rhythm comes into play that attunes their lives to their hearts and lungs. More time is available for their eyes, ears, nose, and imagination to absorb the surrounding scene. They work toward their ambitions and goals at a calmer pace. The world is not merely slower; it is better.

THE OPEN AIR

The value of a slower pace in life was brought home to me in early 1963 when the country flashed through a period of vigor. During the John Kennedy administration a campaign was waged to get the feet of America walking again. The impulse was the fifty-mile walk. *Time* magazine termed the nationwide phenomenon the Kennedy Pace Corps. Teenagers to gray-hairs were urged to get out of their homes and automobiles and join the other fifty-mile marchers to health and vitality. Tens of thousands did, and I was one of them.

The walk literally opened my eyes. For years I had driven my car over the same route from Alhambra to Manhattan Beach in southern California. Since the route was about fifty miles long, I decided to walk the same way by following the frontage roads along the freeways and the sidewalks along the streets that angled through outlying towns and over the hills.

The walk took the entire day, but at the end of the fifty miles I had seen the route as I had never before in all those years. I saw old bookstores, pawnshops, and ethnic restaurants I never knew existed. I saw houses and department-store display windows and fresh-fruit stands. I passed old men gardening their vegetables, teen-agers overhauling their Fords, women shuffling through dresses at a sidewalk sale. I saw them up close, face to face, person to person. I talked to some, waved to others.

I had time to look and absorb. I ran into a couple of girls who knew I didn't belong to their territory and it was something to remember. I walked past an alcoholic derelict sleeping in the doorway of an abandoned walk-up apartment building. "Closed" was chalked on the front door. For the first time I realized that wild lupine and poppies actually grew along the Stocker Street by-pass through the Crenshaw hills. As I approached Manhattan Beach I had time to smell the salt air and notice the change in housing designs near the beach area. It was a revelation.

In short, the route that I had driven at sixty miles per hour was really a different route altogether. The reason: I had time to be part of it.

TIME TO LOOK

It is the same with riding a bike. On the back roads of New Hampshire, I have time to notice the leaf-chewing porcupine barely visible against the dark tree trunks. Woodchucks are easy to spot by the side of the road. I can see the yellow stripe on red-wing blackbirds as well as think only once about stopping to enjoy a long green vista.

In town I have little problem with parking spaces and no problem with gas stations. (On the other hand, towns have problems with cars, which occupy 300 square feet of parking space each; a bike can be parked in ten square feet.) On some afternoons I pedal faster alongside the traffic than all the reined-in horsepower snorting feverishly in congestion— and I'm much happier at home because of it.

A car can carry big loads and be a pleasant way to travel. I drive one frequently. The mistake is to limit choices to the automobile alone. A bike is not only an appropriate means of travel in many situations, it's also extremely enjoyable at the same time, to say nothing of the health benefits of rhythmic exercise for your heart and lungs.

Actually, the automobile was invented as an alternative to the bicycle as well as to the horse and buggy. After 1891 the four-wheelers quickly overtook the two-wheelers in the United States. Today, approximately 100 million cars crowd the cities and roads of this country, nearly one machine for every two people. That may be one reason for the phenomenal rebirth of the saner two-wheeler.

THE EARLY BIKES

The first contraption resembling a bicycle was invented by Chevalier de Sivrac of France in 1791. Over the years the invention passed through many variations and deviations, including one with the front wheel as large as sixty-four inches in diameter and the back wheel as small as twelve inches in diameter. This design was extremely unstable because of the high center of gravity.

In 1879 Harry J. Lawson in England lowered the center of gravity and invented the prototype of the modern machine. He used a smaller front wheel and attached a chain to the rear wheel. This way the same distance was covered by pedaling with a chain, with safety, as with a giant front wheel.

Seven years later fellow countryman James Starley came up with two thirty-inch wheels to stabilize the invention even further.

As with any new, intriguing creation, records had to be set and exotic undertakings undertaken. The first man who traveled around the world on a bike was Thomas Stevens. He left San Francisco on April 22, 1884, and arrived in Boston August 24 of the same year. From Boston he sailed by ship and then continued his bike trip in Europe and Asia.

The first man to cross the United States in under three weeks was Eugene McPherson in 1949. He left Santa Monica, California, and pedaled the 3,054 miles to New York City in 20 days, 4 hours, and 29 minutes.

Competitions grew from individual excursions. The most famous is the Tour de France, first run in 1903. The race covers about 3,120 miles, the most grueling of them passing through the Pyrenees Mountains. Participants take about twenty-one days for the race.

With the mass production of the automobile in the United States, interest in the bicycle dwindled, especially during the 1930s. It revived again during the Second World War, when domestic fuel, steel, and other automobile components were scarce. Then interest in biking dwindled again after the war.

The tide turns once more and the bicycle today is again rising in respect and sales. Bicycle manufacturers have extended their production day and dealers cannot keep up with the demand in sales and service. Unlike the fifty-mile walk, the bicycle boom is not a fad. It comes at (or is symptomatic of) a time when traffic jams are intolerable to commuters, heart disease kills too many sedentary executives, the population grows ever more pollution-aware and ecology-minded, and millions of people are looking to the simple pleasures of life.

BIKEWAYS

Cities and states recognize the trend and are accommodating the influx of bike hikers. Bikeways, where riders can travel on regulated safety routes, are being established across the country. The first one, a twenty-five-mile route, opened in Homestead, Florida, in 1962. Two years later a 300-mile bikeway between La Crosse and Kenosha, Wisconsin, was opened. A 250-mile route was inaugurated with fanfare in 1971 in the Chicago area.

Now more than 15,000 miles of bikeways exist in the country. The U. S. Department of the Interior proposes 100,000 miles of bikeways in its system of parks and recreation land. National parks are to have their share of biking privileges as a means of preserving the natural setting as much as possible while still serving hundreds of thousands of visitors. With an estimated 6,000 government workers riding bicycles to their jobs every day in Washington, D.C., and 10,000 bicyclists in Central Park, New York City, on a sunny day, America is moving with its feet again.

THE 10-SPEED

Tricycles, tandems, unicycles, folding bicycles are available, but the 10-speed lightweight bicycle is the favorite. It's also the most practical and efficient. The derailleur shift for the ten gear ratios (five gears in the rear, two in the front) has been perfected over the years. When properly adjusted, this bicycle transmission has mechanical tolerance enough for the beginner and is virtually foolproof for everyone else.

The 10-speed has made biking more versatile than it was with the older 3-speed bike that was popular one and two decades ago. With little strain, the 10-speed can conquer all but the steepest hills. It can poke along on lazy back roads or cover great distances on flat ground. It can handle a quick trip to the post office or an all-day outing to the woods. It can be carried over the shoulder if need be or piled with camping gear for a weekend sojourn.

The lightness of a good 10-speed bike is matched by its wide range of gears, its compactness, its sturdiness, its ease of handling, its relative low cost of purchase and maintenance, but most of all its riding pleasure. A 3- or 5-speed suffices, but for optimum enjoyment any bike hike begins with a 10-speed.

HIKING

Never let the word "hiking" detract from any of your ideas or enthusiasm for a bike trip. With some of the suggestions from the following chapters applied to your riding, bike hiking can be made pleasant and surprisingly labor-free. Today, with most roads constructed smoothly and safely, with many interesting routes and destinations from which to select, and with simple fundamental planning, hiking across the city or the country on your bike can be a challenging delight.

If biking all the way to a national park, or whatever your destination, is too exhausting and time-consuming, you can buy a fairly inexpensive bike rack that fits onto the back bumper of your car. Attach the bike securely to the rack and you're on your way. Once at Yosemite or Yellowstone or Cape Cod, you have your bike for leisurely rides around the countryside.

Airlines have responded to the bicycle enthusiast, too. Nearly all major airlines accept a bicycle as one piece of luggage. Some airlines crate it themselves. At other airlines you may have to crate your two-wheeler yourself, or at least remove the pedals, turn the front wheel back, attach it snugly to the frame, and turn the handlebars sideways or remove them altogether to reduce the width of the bike.

THINK BIKE

Whichever way you transport your bike, whether it's by bumper rack, train, plane, or pedaling, get into the habit of thinking bike. If you want to get out of the house, ride your bike instead of driving the car. If you feel like browsing through the public library, ride your bike to it. The same goes for picking up a few items at the grocery store, mailing letters, visiting friends, buying magazines, even commuting to work.

The bike habit leads to bike hikes. Soon, small trips to the shoeshop expand to longer trips to a neighboring town. The open road beckons. You take more trips with your bike because the bike habit becomes second nature. You feel better, enjoy the days more, and find that biking, through its side effects, enlivens your outlook and calms your inner self.

Your muscles tone up. Your diaphragm increases its efficiency on your lungs. Your arteries retain their elasticity and your weight is easier to control. You sleep better at night and your energy level is higher than Hoover Dam.

If you and your bike click together in the slightest, in a short time you'll ask yourself why you hadn't rediscovered each other sooner. Probably as a youngster you had a love affair with a bike, but it grew out of favor as the years passed. Now with bicycles becoming more respected as sensible vehicles instead of pacifying toys, all ages are out front again with their loves. *To bike or not to bike?* The answer is obvious.

2

GETTING THE MOST FROM
YOUR MACHINE

Your bicycle is a machine, not a toy. Treat it like one. Let it work for you. Don't you work for it. Enjoy your two-wheeler, but maximize all its design potential so that you use it to full advantage.

For bike hiking the details of caring for your machine are important. The tightening of a screw, the lubricating of movable parts, the straightening of the handlebars, and all the other small adjustments add up to a more secure, pleasant trip. In the long run a well-cared-for machine performs closer to your expectations and provides you with one more measure of safety you can believe in.

FRAME

The core of any bicycle is the frame. Frequently forgotten and neglected, the frame is the basis on which a bike is judged poor, adequate, or superior. A frame with superior tubing, such as Reynolds double-butted 531 or Columbus, combines strength with lightweightness, flexibility with sturdiness.

Before you set out on a trip, check the frame of your bike. Chances are that all will be in order for the lifetime of your bicycle, even on the inexpensive models. Nevertheless, since the frame is the heart of your machine, take the minute and a half to look it over.

Look for tiny cracks in the tubing, especially at the joints. Look for gaps in the welded seams. Check all angles of the lug seams for any kind of separation of the joints, which could be the start of a major break if you happened to run over a curb and create a strong shock to the frame system. Inspect the undersides of the tubing, not merely what is easy to see from the top. Check for cracks on the forks where the wheels are bolted tight.

If you spot any such "disease" of the frame, ask an expert bike mechanic whether the damage is too great for safety. If no mechanic is at hand and you are undecided, decide in favor of yourself and don't ride the bike. Damage to the frame is serious enough to consider purchase of another bike.

TIRES

You get better mileage per output factor of energy if your tires are inflated at all times to the recommended pressure. Remember that all 27 by 1 1/4-inch tires do not call for the same air pressure. At one point I had a front tire that called for seventy pounds of pressure while the back tire called for fifty.

The manufacturer's recommended pressure is embossed on the sides of the tires. Maintain that pressure at all times. If you're carrying weight on your bike, or carrying a surplus of carbohydrates on yourself, add five pounds or so of pressure over the recommended limit. The added pressure is well within the tolerance of a tire blowout and gives you an effortless ride. Underinflated tires drag the bike by squashing more rubber at the point of contact with the pavement. Grossly underinflated tires can snap off the rim and cause an accident.

Carry a bicycle pressure gauge in your pocket or in a seat bag while riding. On very hot days when you're riding over asphalt or letting your bike stand in the sun, check the tire pressure every hour or so. Heat expands the air inside the tires and can cause blowouts. One bike-shop owner I know says that, when he sees a group of bikers congregating on a hot summer day in a park across from his shop, it's just a matter of time before he hears a loud bang and a chagrined biker comes in for a repair job. "All they have to do is check the pressure once in a while," he says. "If it's going up fast, just release some air. It's a lot easier than a patch job."

Inflate your tires with a hand pump. These pumps push air into the tires at slow controllable rates and won't accidentally explode the tire in your face. A gas-station pump can easily blow out a tire—and often does. If you have no choice except to use a gas-station air hose, do so with caution. If the service-station pump has no automatic gauge setting, pump the air into your bike tire in half-second spurts. Check the pressure with your own gauge after each spurt. Gas-station air pumps operate at 200 pounds per square-inch pressure.

Ride on quality tires. One time in an emergency I had to use an imported tire made with third-rate rubber. That very day I skidded to a stop several times and each time a section of rubber burned away like wax. A quality tire, on the other hand, would never melt away so fast. Bike tires should last between 3,000 and 4,000 miles of ordinary travel. No matter how many miles you have on one, be sure to have enough tread to help stop the bike safely on wet streets as well as minimize the chance for punctures and blowouts.

BRAKES

Before every outing, and, in fact, before every time you push off down the street, press the hand brakes to see that they function properly. Never presume on your safety. See that the brake blocks clamp completely on the rims of the wheels for a sure, smooth stop. Test the brakes to be certain that the wheels lock tightly.

Lubricate the working metal parts of the brake system occasionally, but never lubricate the brake blocks themselves. Hand brakes work on friction against the wheel rim. A single drop of oil can cause the brake block to be useless and result in injuries. Some bikers wipe the rims clean of any dirt, street grease, or water before riding. It's a good idea.

Brake blocks come in two different styles. The older style is solid black rubber with a flat surface. The newer style is off-red, made with nodules on the braking surface. Both styles are equally effective and last thousands of miles. The one advantage of the newer model is that, in rainy weather or when riding through a filled gutter, the serrated blocks remove water from the rim faster by allowing the water to filter between the notches. This may be a deciding factor in choosing the newer style if you anticipate riding in much rainy weather.

CHAIN

A gummy, dirty, oil-clogged chain makes a clunker out of your machine. On the other hand, a clean chain operates smoothly and gives you, not a gritty squeak, but a low rhythmic hum of mechanical perfection. That hum of security is worth the time it takes to clean the chain.

You can clean the chain two ways. First, remove the chain with a chain-link tool. Fill a large flat-bottom can or other container with kerosene and soak the chain for about an hour or so. After the sludge is dissolved from the chain, lift the chain to let it drip dry. Then take a nonshredding cloth and wipe it. Put it back on the bike and apply a light coat of WD-40 lubricant or lightweight household oil.

A second way, if you have no chain-link remover, is to clean the chain while it's in place on the bike. The quicker method is to apply some WD-40 to the chain and wipe it off with a rag so that the excess sludge comes off too.

A more time-consuming way is to rub an old toothbrush in and out of each chain link and collect the sludge with tissue paper or rag. Use the rubber tip of the toothbrush to poke the dirt from the crevices and centers of the links. This takes time, perhaps twenty minutes or half an hour, but it is the next best way to soaking the chain in kerosene.

A bicycle chain is extremely strong. It's a rare case when one breaks. However, taking care of it by removing the dirt and grime picked up on the road helps reduce the time the chain takes to stretch and corrode. Also, remember to apply an extremely light coat of oil to the chain. It needs very little lubrication to function well. Excess oil absorbs dust from the air and turns it into greasy dirt. You'll have to reclean it that much sooner.

SADDLE

The most effective seat for bike hiking is the narrow racing style. It is carefully designed to transfer to the bike the utmost energy your body can develop. The slim front half of the seat allows unhampered movement of your thighs as you pedal. As a result, no energy is lost by rubbing against the saddle. The hardness of the racing seat reverberates the energy from your gluteus maximus and thighs back through your legs to the pedals, thereby gaining additional power for you.

The mattress seat, the other popular style, has springs to absorb the reaction energy from your legs. This energy is continually and forever lost. The mattress seat is flatter, wider, and springier than the racing style. It appears more comfortable than the racing saddle and actually may be at first. However, in the long run the mattress seat sponges away your strength and becomes annoying, to say the least, and defeating, to say the worst. I've tried both on outings and the racing seat wins.

If you switch from a mattress to a racing saddle, give the new seat about 200–300 miles of riding before it contours to your body. You can help the softening of the hard leather by occasionally applying linseed oil or Vaseline to the underside of the seat. Avoid putting the oil on the top or it may rub off on your pants. Some bikers break in a new saddle by bending the leather back and forth with their fingers once a day and by hitting it periodically with a broom handle.

Saddles do come with padding sewn in them, but if the padding is too thick the net effect in energy lost is like the mattress spring seat. Hard, stretched leather is the best. The racing seats made of plastic work, but be prepared for this type to break in *your* seat instead of the reverse.

DROP HANDLEBARS

The Maes, or racing-style, handlebars, as opposed to the touring, or flat style, are by far the more effective. The drop bars offer you four basic riding grips. All of them give you more power by demanding that your back and stomach muscles as well as your arms and shoulders work. The flat handlebars do not require you to use all these muscles. Consequently, you rely almost entirely on only your legs.

The drop bars also force your body into a C position, with your back and shoulders hunched over. This reduces wind resistance considerably. Besides that, the hunched-over position makes it much easier to climb hills. I've climbed the same hills with both style handlebars and found that the racing bars are half again as effective as the flat style.

TOE CLIPS

Studies show that as much as one third more energy can be regained from your foot action if toe clips are strapped to your feet. With your feet semirigid on the pedals, the backswing of your foot can be used for power instead of free-riding on the strength of the downswing of your other foot. You can apply pressure to the pedal the entire revolution by pulling up with your foot in the toe clip.

Toe clips are essential on bike hikes of moderate to maximum distance. Too often they are overlooked or thought to be designed for professional racers alone. Not true. A set of toe clips is inexpensive and absolutely necessary to achieve full pedaling power.

The clips, which come in several sizes, are thin aluminum strips bent in a U shape. They are bolted to the fronts of rat-trap pedals. Be sure to fit the toe clips so that the balls, not the insteps, of your feet rest on the centers of the pedals. This is the recommended position for full power. If your set doesn't fit correctly, adjust the position of the toe clip with a series of washers or nuts when you secure them to the pedals.

The straps for the toe clips keep your feet snugly in place.

They also transfer energy to the pedal that might be lost when the sides of your feet are pressed outward, especially during hard pedaling uphill. Some riders have problems with the claustrophobia of being locked into the bike and fear disaster in emergencies if they can't get their feet free of the pedals fast enough. For the fearful, the metal clips can be used without the straps and still keep the feet in place. Clips alone still conserve energy without "locking in" the rider. Used with or without the straps, toe clips are essential for bike hikes.

SHIFTING GEARS

The art of shifting can be learned by anybody. A smooth, noiseless shift from one gear to another, or from the front derailleur to the rear, requires practice and a closeness with your bike. Bicycles have different feels and it takes some riding time before the two of you become a locomotive unit.

The fundamental rule in using the gears is never to ride in a gear that drags, one that takes more energy to pump than necessary. Biking should be as effortless as possible. Any gear that requires your legs to strain so that the exertion is noticeable and saps your energy should be a sign that you're in the wrong gear. You should be in a lower one.

Being in the wrong gear is most noticeable on upgrades or hills. Always shift to a lower gear when approaching a hill. Shift before the hill, not once you're on it. On a 5- or 10-speed bike, you must pedal slowly as you shift. This becomes difficult, and sometimes impossible, if you are already straining uphill. In this situation go back downhill in order to have free pedaling time to shift.

The best technique is to shift slowly and smoothly. Pedal easily as you carefully, unhurriedly, pull back the gear lever. Reduce the pressure in your legs and the speed of the revolutions, but continue the pedaling. This reduction allows the chain to slip onto the next gear sprocket without clanking or straining. With careful, slow shifting and riding time for practice, you are soon able to move from one gear to the next with ease, as if you were moving through soapy water.

The derailleur system of gears is designed for "feel" rather than for exact positions. This is a safety feature so that you can keep your eyes on the road. It requires practice to know the area on the lever for second gear or for eighth, but skill in shifting gears substitutes for strength in your legs. Develop that skill and you'll have good, hard-riding days when you're tired but never fatigued.

CADENCE

Directly associated with shifting is the cadence you develop in riding. The cadence, or number of revolutions you pedal per minute, is entirely up to you. Some bikers cruise along on sixty-five revolutions per minute, others churn up the highways with ninety-five. Professional and amateur bicycle racers can move on 100 rpms for hours at a time, sometimes all day, and then increase their output toward the finish of a race when the competition does likewise.

The cadence you set for yourself, or rather the one that evolves from your riding habits, is largely determined by your physical condition and temperament. The important consideration is that you continue your cadence in each gear you use. In other words, if you've set a cadence of seventy revolutions per minute in fourth gear, you should approximate that pace when you're in eighth gear. This is one of the reasons for multiple gears on a bike. Maintaining a set cadence establishes a rhythm in your legs and your energy output that is best used if not interrupted or knocked off balance. The gears do the hard work, not your legs.

In bike hiking, as in mountain hiking, a brisk rhythm is best. Poking along at sixty revolutions per minute is not as relaxing as it appears. A slow pace can be boring and turn you sluggish. A good seventy to seventy-five revolutions per minute is a solid all-around pace. Better yet is eighty to ninety, well within any biker's reach after some time on the road and command in shifting gears.

You can test your cadence by counting the revolutions of your legs as you move along. Count the seconds to yourself this way: one thousand and one, one thousand and two, one thousand and three, and so forth. At the same time figure how many times your right leg has made a complete circle within the framework of the seconds you're counting. For example, if you're pedaling one and a half times every second, you're moving at ninety revolutions per minute.

A GOOD FIT

Fitting your bike to your body increases power output and eliminates aches and pains. The world abounds with all sorts of formulas designed to match the average bicycle with the average body, like the formula that specifies that a bike-frame size should be the length of the rider's leg from heel to crotch minus ten inches. Too bad some people have long legs and short torsos or short legs and long torsos. The formulas are good to know in general, but they should be regarded as guides, not gods.

Fit *your* body to *your* bike. Basically, you should be able to straddle the top tube with both your feet on the ground. This is not enough though. Seats and handlebars are adjustable and should be adjusted if they are uncomfortable and give you less than the most efficient power output.

Adjust your seat so that when you're on the bike your left knee bends no more than about an inch and a half when your left heel on the pedal is nearest the ground. At the same time tilt the front of the saddle up about an inch so that the seat slants down toward the back wheel. Also, set the seat back horizontally to the point where your arms are straight when your hands are on the handlebars. This combination of positions of your saddle provides the maximum use of your leg muscles and the most comfortable position for your arms.

Adjust your handlebars so that the top of the stem is approximately about an inch below the top of the saddle. For bikers with extra-long arms, insert a handlebar stem extension. The additional two or three inches forward eliminates the crimping of your elbows. The handlebars are lower than the saddle so that you can lean into them and apply a forward thrust with your shoulders and chest. Wind resistance is also reduced.

KEEP IN CONDITION

As marvelous and ingenious a design as the bicycle is, it does not move any farther or faster than you are prepared to pedal it. When you come to the limit of your physical endurance, your trip stops for the day.

To sustain a ride and to enjoy it more, keep yourself in top physical condition. You are the fuel of your machine. It is up to you to provide the reserve of power. The only way to achieve this is gradually to build up a power source by conditioning your muscles for bike riding. Make your goal endurance, not merely speed.

As all athletes know, each sport utilizes a combination of muscles different from other sports. Football requires different conditioning from basketball. Bicycling uses a different combination of muscles from swimming, so different in fact that bicycle racers cannot mix bicycling and swimming. Conditioning for one counteracts conditioning for the other.

For the ordinary biker, the best conditioning is simply to ride a bike. For best results, set a pattern of riding. Make it a habit. Ride an hour before school or work. Ride an hour after school or work. If you're planning a fairly long trip, ride every day. Know the distances from your home to your destination so that you can judge your progress in time and conditioning.

One program for conditioning might be:

First Week

Monday: 5 miles in 1 hour.
Add 1 mile each day.
Saturday: 10 miles in 1 hour.

Second Week

Monday: 10 miles in 1 hour.
Add 1 mile each day.
Saturday: 15 miles in 1 hour 15 minutes.

Third Week

Monday: 15 miles in 1 hour 15 minutes.
Add 1 mile each day.
Saturday: 20 miles in 2 hours.

Fourth Week

Monday: 20 miles in 2 hours.
Add 1 mile each day.
Saturday: 25 miles in 2 1/2 hours.

On rainy days indoor exercises such as pedaling an imaginary bicycle while lying on the floor are good. Other exercises, such as running and calisthenics, develop larger breathing capacity, tighten the muscles, and attune the heart to increased beating, but these exercises are substitutes. Nothing is identical to your legs putting pressure on pedals, your arms pulling on the handlebars for an uphill climb, or your back and stomach muscles working on an extended drive on flat open road. You can't avoid it. Preparation for bike hiking must be made on a bike.

Normally, you breathe about sixteen times each minute. Riding a bike quickly increases this rate by three or four times in order to supply oxygen to your working muscles. To sustain this rapid breathing without pain in your ribs, you must train regularly to develop breathing habits and greater capacity. The quadriceps, or thigh, muscles, your major power source, cannot function without great quantities of oxygen.

Just as your muscles fuel your bike, so does your diet fuel your muscles. Bicycling produces amazing effects on your health, your complexion, your attitude, and your spirit. So go all the way by eating well. Avoid fats and fried foods. Stay away from the cream puffs and chocolate eclairs. Get your sugar from dates, figs, grapes, and other energy-packed fruits. Make bicycling part of all aspects of your life rather than merely a detour of the day.

MAKE IT SHINE

Every time I clean my bike it goes faster. Or seems to.
Some bikers in the world deliberately let their bikes look like
an accident. Apparently this ploy is to ward off the bicycle-
thieving pirates of our urban society. However, the question
is not to have a bike that discourages others from stealing it
but to enjoy it and make the days first-rate for yourself.

Make your two-wheeler shine. Wax the rims. Wipe off
the frame. Clean the derailleurs. It'll feel lighter, go faster,
and work better because your bright classy machine makes
you feel better.

Then it's time for the two of you, bike and body, to ride as
a unit, to get to know each other so that your legs become an
extension of the pedals and your arms become an extension
of the handlebars. You and your bike join forces. You unify
the best of both of you. That's when you get the most from
your machine.

3

WHERE TO GO AND WHAT TO TAKE

Except for the moon, bike riders can go just about anywhere. They can go to the county park or around the world, which Ray Reece of England did a couple of years ago. They can bike up and down neighborhood hills or over the Rocky Mountains. The choice depends on interest, time, and personal conditioning.

The fun of bike hiking is as rich for a trip to the city arboretum as it is for a four-state, month-long excursion. Keep all possibilities open. If you would like to try an overnight trip but are hesitant about the distance, take a couple of one-day trips first. Work up to the big one. If the big one doesn't interest you, don't ignore the many possibilities for destinations close-by.

By all means get out on the open road, no matter how far you travel. Biking to nearby sites and scenes is an invigorating family adventure as well as a pleasant day for those who like to ride alone.

Here are some possible destinations:

PICNIC TRIPS

These four- or five-hour trips are ideal to make a day pleasant without being exhausting. Plan these so that you leave home in midmorning, arrive at your destination at about noon.

eat lunch, relax and enjoy the surroundings, see what there is to see, and then head back home. The rest of the day is yours. On top of that you're feeling exhilarated and at ease with the bike riding.

Parks	Fishing holes
Arboretums	Picturesque bridges
Museums	Colleges and universities
Zoos	Dams
Marinas	Rivers
Beaches	Lakes
Memorials	Campgrounds
Historical sites	Famous cemeteries

You need only the bare essentials to take along on a short picnic trip. It's doubtful that a picnic site takes you far from where you can quickly find emergency help if you need it.

A small saddlebag or a box with a lid strapped down to a carrier rack on the back wheel should haul both your picnic supplies and what little gear you need. Whatever you do, travel light. Think ahead carefully. Even on these short trips, take only what you absolutely need.

Checklist for Picnic Trips

Tube-repair kit	Water jug
Screwdriver	Hat
Six-inch crescent wrench	Sunglasses
Pliers	Pocketknife
Air pump	First-aid kit
Tire irons	

DAY-LONG TRIPS

Day-long trips offer more leeway for combining a bike ride with sightseeing. If you take an entire day to bike to a destination, to make a tour of the site you've selected, and then bike home, you should plan in detail your route and time schedule.

Usually, a day-long trip is within the area you're familiar

with. Nevertheless, take a map of the area and study it carefully. Your route is important. Plan one that makes a loop
with your home as starting and finishing point. With a circular
route you won't have to return over the same territory you
traveled during the morning. Such a trip is more interesting.

A circular route also allows you to take advantage of the
wind. Which way the wind blows depends on your particular
locale. A call to the local weather service can provide you
with that exact information. In some parts of the country,
the wind blows from the east in the morning and then
from the west in the afternoon. In some locales the wind
always blows in one direction. Find out about your area.

By knowing the general wind direction you can plan your
trip so that you return with the wind at your back. Traveling
against the wind in the morning when you're fresh and vi-
brant with energy is far easier than fighting it on the last leg
of your day. Route your trip accordingly.

Take hills into consideration, too. A slight upgrade in a
car can be an arduous climb on a bicycle. Study the local map
and match the roads to your destination with the knowledge
you have of the area. If the hills can't be avoided, then plan
the trip so that you face the big uphills in the morning on the
way to your destination while you're fresh. If the majority
of the hills in the afternoon are downhills, you slap yourself
on the back in congratulation for your foresight.

Here are some possibilities for longer trips:

Neighboring towns	Famous graveyards
Waterfalls	Hilltop views
Harbors and shipyards	Farms
Famous churches	Piers
Art colonies	Observatories and
Lighthouses	planetariums
Special libraries	Art galleries
Tours (wineries, factories,	Bird and wildlife
historical sites)	sanctuaries

Bike gear to take on day-long trips is nearly the same as
for short picnic trips. The chance of your getting into deep
trouble on a one-day excursion is slight. Again, the bare es-

sentials are all that you need. Foam-rubber pillows, extra riding jerseys, and the other luxuries add needless weight, the biking burr that can make any trip a chore.

Checklist for Day-long Trips

Tube-repair kit	Aspirin
Screwdriver	Windbreaker
Six-inch crescent wrench	Friction tape
Pliers	Two water jugs
Air pump	Hat
First-aid kit	Sunglasses
Pocketknife	Maps
Paper towels	Tire irons

OVERNIGHT TRIPS

Overnight trips call for the most time, energy, and detailed planning of all, but the sense of accomplishment and enjoyment is comparable to such large undertakings. Careful attention must be given to the selection of supplies and route. Bikers on the road for long-range trips should be as self-sufficient and self-reliant as possible and should know exactly where they are going and how to get there. Turning onto the wrong highway and discovering the mistake two miles down the road can be extremely frustrating. No biker likes to retreat when all that energy could have been channeled in the right direction.

BY CAR

Bikers are discovering that by combining the car with their two-wheelers they can have a multidimensional vacation. Metal bike racks, relatively inexpensive to purchase or easy to make at home, can be latched to the back bumper of a car to carry one or two bicycles. One design is the Bike Toter, which sells for about $20 from Santa Monica, California. Other racks are designed to carry bikes over the passenger compartment.

Another alternative is less expensive and less permanent for those who don't want an empty bike rack bolted to the car all the time. Stretch ropes made of rubber, with hooks on the ends, can secure a bike to a rear bumper without worry. Many times I have propped my 10-speed against the back bumper of my Volkswagen, tied it down with three stretch ropes, placed cardboard at the three or four spots where the bike rested on the car, and driven off down the road without the slightest difficulty.

One time the same stretch ropes came in handy for another biker I saw on the road. He was having trouble with a wobbly back wheel and had stopped by the side of the highway to fix it. I stopped and we exchanged biking tricks of the trade. He wasn't making much headway with his repairs so I offered to get him out of the difficulty. We tied his bike down on the back bumper with the three stretch ropes I had in my car and drove ten miles to the nearest bike shop for repairs. The ropes made me a friend, who continued his trip from Connecticut to Maine and back.

BY BUS

Transporting a bicycle by car is far from the only means of getting to distant glories. Trains, buses, and airplanes all accept bicycles, though bus drivers sometimes have to be persuaded that your machine won't destroy their kingdoms. Little Caesars they are at times. One biker I know had a run-in with a driver in Dallas, Texas. He wanted to get to Fort Worth, bought a ticket, and had his bike ready to load. The driver saw the weird contraption and said absolutely no. Words flew back and forth because the biker had transported his bike on other buses of the same line. The driver won that round. A little later, a more sympathetic driver on the next scheduled bus out of town said he couldn't care less whether the bike was packaged or not as long as it could fit and didn't damage the other baggage. If you find yourself in a similar situation, the lesson is: don't despair after one rejection. Tell your story to the dispatcher or manager or another more receptive driver.

The basic problem is that bicycles as baggage have a short history in the transportation business. That's the reason bicycles are listed among other exotic paraphernalia. The offi-

cial Continental baggage regulations, for example, state that
the maximum baggage weight is 150 pounds per adult ticket.
Nothing over twenty-four inches in height, twenty-four inches
in width, and forty-five inches in length is accepted. The code
further stipulates that "to comply with the laws and regulations and for your protection, the following items will not be
accepted as baggage: acids, go-carts, bicycles, cylinders con-
taining compressed gas, explosives, fireworks, gases, guns (see
agent for exceptions), poisons . . ." and other items. Apparently, bicycles are dangerous weapons. Don't believe it.

BY TRAIN

Transporting a bike by train is no problem and is not expensive. The charge is one or two dollars, depending on the
distance. No crating is necessary. Groups I know of personally have put their bikes on Amtrak in Los Angeles (the old
Santa Fe line), boarded the passenger section, and ridden to
Flagstaff, Arizona. There they disembarked, retrieved their
bikes from the depot, mounted their steeds, and pedaled the
fifty-five miles to the Grand Canyon. From all accounts, it
was a stupendous trip.

BY PLANE

Transporting your bicycle by plane is also painless. The
charge as excess baggage is $7.00. Different airlines have
different regulations. Some, like United, have boxes available
in which to crate the bike. Others, like American, have
heavy-duty plastic bags in which the bike is inserted and the
bag tied shut.

Generally, all that is required is removing the pedals and
turning the handlebars sideways. If possible, do these two
little tasks at home before you get to the airport. It's also a
good idea to remove any pointed or sharp gadgets on your
bike, items like horns or bells or any excessively protruding
racks. At the same time, remove all loose supplies such as the
air pump, water jugs, saddlebags, handlebar bags, anything
that can easily fall off in the handling of your bike.

Using a combination of car, train, bus, or plane and your

bike is often an ideal way to see country and sites by bicycle that you don't have the time, or energy, to travel the entire distance to on two legs. In fact, in the future it may even be absolutely necessary to travel this way. More national parks are closing the main attraction areas to the automobile and allowing only bicycles as the major personal vehicle. Yosemite, which in the past had grown so clogged and "diseased" with cars, is one that the National Park Service is attempting to rejuvenate as a place of beauty and the bicycle. Cars no longer are permitted on the valley floor. Buses, walking, and bicycles are allowed.

I've tried all three forms of public transportation in moving my bike and me together and have had little trouble with agents and no problems with damage. A telephone call to your local bus, train, or plane office can provide you with exact details suited to your destination and locale as well as inform you about what is required of you to prepare your bike for shipment. Whatever is necessary is more than compensated for on the other end of your trip when you have your bike there with you to enjoy.

For these longer overnight trips, here are a few suggestions:

State parks	Across the country
National parks	To the Canadian or Mexican
Ghost towns	border
Beaches	Following a river
Coast highway routes	To the Mississippi River
Wildlife sanctuaries	State capitals
Resorts	Neighboring states

The selection of gear to take along on an overnight trip is important both for what you take as well as how much weight it entails. Certain items are necessary whether you're going the deluxe motel and coffee-shop circuit or the pine-tree and campfire route. Either way, thirty pounds of gear should be the limit.

Whatever sleeping sites you choose, the criterion to base your gear selection on is a combination of efficiency and lightweightness, with heavy emphasis on lightweight. You can improvise a tool or fix a problem with ingenuity if you don't have the correct wrench size in your bag, but you can't reduce the weight of your gear unless you get rid of the items altogether. Remember, compactness is not lightweightness, though to have a slim cargo on your machine is rewarding in traffic and narrow roads.

Shop around for the lightest, most compact, most efficient gear for its size and design. For example, the flashlight in the glove compartment of your car is probably seven or eight inches long and weighs close to three quarters of a pound. A Mallory light, on the other hand, is an extremely lightweight flashlight that fits in the palm of your hand, projects a strong light 250 feet, and weighs less than a fat apple.

The first-aid kit that you buy at the drugstore is packaged for selling, not for bike riding. The container encloses a lot of wasted space. Be smart. Take the contents of the kit out of the standard container, wrap a rubber band around them, and slip them inside a small plastic bag. You probably can shrink the carrying space three times in addition to ridding yourself of the two or three ounces the container weighs.

Don't scoff at eliminating an ounce here and an ounce there. If you don't get rid of all the ounces you can, you find too late, on the road, that those unnecessary extra ounces add up to extravagant pounds and sore legs. Good bikers should follow the example of the long tradition of good mountain hikers. One climber I know goes so far as to measure out the amount of salt he plans to use for each meal and then puts it in a plastic bag. That way he can leave the salt boxes at home.

Some tube-repair kits are packaged in a half-empty can that is useless on a long bike hike. Remove the contents and repackage and label them. Buy the smallest package of any item you need, the smallest insect repellent (Cutter's is best), the smallest suntan lotion for cheeks, nose, and ears (Sea and Ski $\frac{7}{16}$ ounce tube is perfect), the smallest, lightest sleeping bag (a two-pound, down, mummy bag is ideal). We're in the age of miniaturization. Quality sporting goods and ordinary household items follow suit with lightweight, streamlined designs, but you have to shop around for them. Quality products pay dividends in an easier, more pleasant trip.

Checklist for Overnight Trips

MOTELS

Tube-repair kit
Pliers
Six-inch crescent wrench
Screwdriver (Phillips and blade)
Two water jugs
First-aid kit
Aspirin
Air pump
Two shirts
Two underpants
Hat
Windbreaker
Plastic raincoat
Swiss army pocketknife
Saddlebags
Shaving kit
Toothbrush
Comb
Suntan lotion
One long-sleeve, medium-weight shirt
Toothpaste
Bike lubricant
Odometer
Bicycle lock
Spoke wrench
Nail pullers
Ben-Gay
Sunglasses
Air-pressure gauge
Maps
Tire irons
Toe clips
Bicycle shoes
Money
Nylon cord
Friction tape
Plastic bags

CAMPING

All of the above plus:

Flashlight
Waterproof matches
One cup
One pot
Tent
Dishcloth
Sweater
Campknife
Scouring pads
Soap
Sleeping bag
Air mattress
Food
One white-gas stove
Knife, fork, spoon
White gas
Insect repellent
Paper towels
Pillowcase for storing food
Collapsible canteen

Optional Equipment

Spare tube
Four spare spokes
Spare gear cable
Candles
Paperback to read
Dog repellent (Halt)
Notebook
Pencil
Halazone tablets to
   purify water

One set spare brake blocks
"Emergency" blanket
Riding gloves
Various extra nuts and bolts
Extra jeans
Salt tablets
Snake-bite kit
Bicycle repair manual
Camera

TOOLS

In thousands of miles of riding the road I have never needed more than a six-inch adjustable crescent wrench, combination Phillips and blade screwdriver, pliers, tire irons, and spoke wrench. These tools have tightened, loosened, adjusted, and repaired all that had to be done on the road. A fancy $15 bicycle tool kit with individual crescent wrenches, T-wrenches, chain-link remover, and the rest, I found, are unnecessary and create excess weight and bulk.

A personal tool kit is good to overhaul your bike at home, but the chances of anything drastically going wrong on the road are extremely slight. A bicycle chain, for example, may stretch and slip over the gear teeth occasionally, but a loose chain can be spotted before the trip and repaired. It is highly unlikely you will need a chain-link remover on a trip, even a thousand-mile excursion. The same goes for the many specialized tools you can buy, such as dog-bone wrenches, that are sold as the one miracle tool but are really inadequate.

Think in terms of riding with only the absolutely essential first-aid tools, not the ones a bicycle mechanic uses or even all the tools you use at home. If (first) something goes wrong, (second) the bike is totally inoperable, and (third) you don't have the proper tool (a highly unlikely combination of events), you can always borrow one, invent one, or thumb a ride to a bike shop.

SADDLEBAGS

Sometimes called "panniers," saddlebags are tied and fitted to an aluminum carrier rack that is bolted to the back fork. They hang down on both sides of the back wheel.

For best long-range results, use bags that are specially designed for bicycles. Avoid bags that are designed for mountain climbing or book carrying on campus. Instead, look for saddlebags that are lightweight, waterproof or water repellent, zippered, easy to pack and unpack, sturdy, and, most important, strongly sewn in the seams. Many times I have passed bikers on the road who complained that their saddlebags were ripping at the seams, a mild disaster if suddenly the bags rip completely from the bike and spill the contents on the highway. Good examples of superior all-around saddlebags are the Bellweather models.

When you choose your saddlebags, do so with Parkinson's Law in mind. Just as work expands to fill the time allotted to it, so does the number of items to fill saddlebags. Choose the medium or smaller size bags, never the largest one. You merely end up stuffing the bag with as much gear as possible. After all, the room is there.

Trick yourself. A smaller size bag forces you to be highly selective in the size and number of your supplies, a choice that pays dividends galore on the road. Even if you plan to camp along the way, the smaller saddlebags have ample room for your gear. Merely plan and pack judiciously.

HANDLEBAR BAG

Too many of the front bags are large and bulky. They block visibility of the front wheel and, because they are so large, allow too much weight to be put in them. In turn, they sometimes make steering shaky and unsafe in tight situations.

Some bikers never use a handlebar bag. However, a small bag in front is handy for supplies (air-pressure gauge, fruit, maps) that are used often on the trip. Probably the best design for bicycles is the Sologne handlebar bag made in

France. It opens from the biker's side while he's on the bike. That way you can remain straddled on the bike as you flip the flap away from you and easily get inside the bag. The other bags open with the lid coming back toward you as you sit on the bike, thus making it more cumbersome to get at the contents. This feature of the French bag is worth the money (about $8.00). It saves you time and eliminates nuisance. While riding you can open the bag to look at maps or stuff your escaping hat inside as you zoom downhill. The lid of the bag is closed with an elastic tie hooked around the stem of the steering column. Whatever bag you choose, aim for a small one.

AIR PUMP

Air pumps at gas stations are designed for automobile tires, not bike tires. Always use a hand air pump designed for bicycles. They are essential. More important, a *good* air pump is essential. Get one that is strong and solid, one that stands up to dropping on the pavement and still remains in working condition. Once I tried to get away with an inexpensive pump. As it happened, I ran into trouble with traffic and the pump fell off the bike onto the asphalt. The pump appeared all right, but two days later on a long country stretch I discovered a slow leak in my front wheel. I stopped to fill it up and further discovered that the air pump was useless. That was bad enough. A full-fledged puncture would have been worse. Buy a good, solid, strong air pump. I did, finally.

ODOMETER

The low monotonous clicking of an odometer drives some bikers up the wall, if not up the hill. Personally, I find an odometer, or mileage indicator, useful in computing the day's ride or how many miles remain to travel to a given destination.

An odometer also can be used to determine the average speed on a trip. For example, if you know from your odometer that you have traveled fifty miles in five hours, you therefore rode at a speed of ten miles per hour. Divide the five hours into the fifty miles to give you the number of miles traveled in one hour.

The English-made odometer is metal, the Japanese model is plastic. Both work well. The clicking is well within mental tolerance range. The main component is attached to the front fork and the "clicking" mechanism is attached to a spoke, which, as it turns, revolves a friction wheel on the main component that adds up the distance. Both the English and Japanese models are computed in tenths of miles. Be sure to purchase an odometer designed for your size wheel. If you have a twenty-seven-inch wheel, get an odometer designed for that size or else the computation will be inaccurate.

An odometer, small and lightweight, is sufficient for your travels. Forget a speedometer. They're bulky, heavy, and unnecessary.

NAIL PULLERS

Whether you're riding on tubular or clincher tires, these gadgets help clear the tires of rocks, glass, nails, and tacks before the evil intruders cut through the rubber and damage the tube. Nail pullers are attached to the bike by loosening the main outer screw of each brake mechanism, slipping the nail puller on, and tightening the screw again. A metal loop then rests on the tire and knocks off the glass and nails as the wheel turns. They're easy to install and they provide you with an extra dose of security.

RIDING GLOVES

Bicycle riding gloves are designed to give you padding on the palms of your hands where you normally grip the handlebars. The gloves, like golf gloves, come only to the second knuckles, leaving the majority of each finger free. They snap tight at the wrist. The better gloves are made of leather on the palm side and knitting on the backside of the hand to allow air flow to the skin.

Riding gloves can help eliminate perspiration that causes

a slippery grip. On the other hand, gloves can also accelerate the time in which your fingers turn numb by cutting off the circulation of blood. Gloves do not have a high priority of importance. If you do want them, buy a good pair. They do protect your hands if you fall to the ground.

SHOES

The best bicycling shoes are the ones racers use. They're lightweight, leather, usually black, have scores of air holes punched through the tops and sides, and have flat hard soles. They are also the most expensive. If you take biking seriously, these are the ones to have. If you take biking seriously and don't have the money to spend so lavishly, but do plan extended trips, shop around for substitutes.

Look for shoes that have hard soles to withstand rat-trap pedals. Look, too, for shoes with no heel to catch on the pedals. Ordinary tennis shoes or sneakers are not totally satisfactory. The pedals eventually wear hard on the soft rubber soles and give you sore feet. You can get away with soft rubber shoes but aim for the best.

HAT

Always wear a hat. It protects your head from constant exposure to the sun and prevents headaches and sunstrokes. The most versatile hats for biking are those made entirely of soft, pliant material like cotton. White tennis hats with green on the insides of the visors that completely encircle the head are good. The visor keeps the sun out of your eyes and off of portions of your neck. The green reduces the glare of sun on your eyes. This type of hat can be soaked in water and worn as a do-it-yourself air conditioner.

CLOTHES

The clothes you wear while riding should protect your energy resources while permitting you optimum comfort. Wear cut-offs or shorts, especially those that are lightweight with smooth seams. Full-length jeans restrict your leg move-ment and waste power. Even cut-off jeans sometimes irritate your seat by the constant rubbing of the thick seams.

Always wear a shirt (girls included). Choose one that is long-sleeved and medium weight. A shirt retains body mois-ture that otherwise blows away with the wind. An unlined nylon windbreaker over the shirt is added protection against dehydration without increasing the discomfiture of too many clothes. On the surface, wearing no shirt, or merely a halter, is appealing, but in the long run it saps energy.

Keep your waist free and flexible. Don't tie sweaters around your middle or your blood circulation will be crimped. Wear belts loosely. Avoid belts with large brass buckles. The flow of blood from heart to hips must be unencumbered.

Cotton or light wool socks keep your feet moist and com-fortable. On extended trips, one change of socks, underwear, and T-shirt is all that's necessary. Wear one set while the second set is drying after you wash them. A pair of long pants or jeans is convenient to have along for changing at night, especially if you're camping. A light sweater under-neath your tightly woven nylon windbreaker is all you need for the chilly windy nights around the campfire. Also, you should be able to get along with only your bike shoes. A second pair of shoes adds much weight and bulk. Remember to keep your clothes to a minimum. They're bulky and quickly increase the pounds.

In cooler weather wear layers of thin clothes, not one large sweater or one heavy jacket or one extra-thick wool shirt. Air is the best insulation. The air between layers of clothes protects you from the cold the best of all. Eskimos learned this millennia ago. Bikers take heed.

LOCK

More than 500,000 bikes were stolen in California in 1971, a 500 per cent increase over 1970. Calling this intolerable, which it is, doesn't prevent a theft, but it does prompt you to keep an eye at all possible times on your bike. Also, registering your bike with the local police does increase the chance of return if it's stolen. Unfortunately, the recovery rate on bicycles is only about 20 per cent. One thief who admitted stealing and selling 300 bicycles said, "The only sure way to protect your bicycle is to keep it with you every minute."

On a bike trip you should keep your machine in sight virtually at all times. No lock dissuades a determined pirate. Metal cutters can snap nearly every chain lock on the market, with the exception of expensive, heavy-duty iron monsters. Keep in mind the trite exaggeration that a twenty-pound bike with a twenty-pound chain lock equals a forty-pound haul up the next hill.

However, it is wise to carry a small, plastic-covered chain lock, not as the ultimate deterrent to experienced thieves, but as a visible restraint for the casual crook, the joy-rider who preys on the easy victims.

Be aware that many bicycles are stolen, but don't let the paranoia of a possible theft of your bike dominate your mind, ruin your trip, or weigh your bike down with iron. Just stay close to your machine. If you go into a coffee shop, park your bike against the front window. Bring it into the front of a grocery store. Ask someone to watch it as you shop for supplies. The best lock is your eyes. Staying close to your machine is the most effective safeguard. It's your pride and joy. It's also your way out of the wilderness, wherever you are.

SPARE PARTS

Spare parts for the bike are good to a point, but don't be overinsured. The cost in bulk and weight is extravagant. Unless you are rough in shifting gears or occasionally throw your bike to the ground on its chain-wheel side, you should never need such things as spare gear cables, spare brake cables, or spare toe clips.

A few selected nuts and bolts that fit such components as the rack over the back wheel, the axle, the brake-block clamps, the toe clips are sufficient. Don't overload yourself with the makings of half another bike. Careful handling and riding of the bike, plus periodic checking, tightening, and adjusting, substitute for the panic reaction of taking too many spare parts that won't be used.

WATER JUGS

Trips that take you away from easily accessible water sources dictate two water jugs instead of the usual one. The jugs fit snugly on the down tube and seat tube. Riding a bike generates friction and heat in your legs, arms, stomach, back, neck, and torso. Water is absolutely necessary to cool your body as you ride.

Drink in small quantities each time but drink often. Don't wait until your mouth is dry. It's getting to be too late then. With such continuous work as pedaling your machine for miles at a time, your cooling system demands constant upkeep and attention. Having two water jugs along guarantees this attention.

You can stave off the plastic taste of the water in your jugs with Kool-Aid. Mix a package (you don't need sugar) in each jug and let it sit overnight. Rinse out the Kool-Aid the following morning so that none of the coloring remains. Then fill the jugs with fresh water. A slight residue of Kool-Aid taste remains in the jugs for about three days and is more pleasant than the clammy taste of plastic.

SLEEPING BAG

If you're camping, you definitely need a sleeping bag. The lightest weight are the best and the most expensive. However, a two-pound goose (not duck) down bag keeps you warmer than a five-pound wool bag. The fluffier insulation of air does the trick. The difference in weight between down and wool is worth the money.

Down bags can also be rolled tighter and smaller than wool, cotton, or Dacron bags. The rip-resistent nylon shells are much lighter, too, than the canvas coverings. A good sleeping bag can be rolled into a ball that easily fits on the top of the rear carrier rack and can be strapped securely by two stretch ropes crossed perpendicularly.

SALT TABLETS

Muscles need salt to function properly. A larger supply of salt is needed when the muscles are in motion continuously, as they are in bike riding. Salt tablets, available at most drugstores or sporting-goods stores, are often the answer to regenerating an unsuspecting biker after he has suffered a mysterious fatigue disproportionate to what he expected. Hot sunny days take away body salt along with perspiration.

Some bikers need less salt than others. One way to maintain an adequate salt level is simply to dash more sodium chloride onto your food. If you're eating at coffee shops, wet your fingers and pour salt on the tips and lick it off. Do this every time you stop to eat and you probably won't have to worry about carrying a package of tablets.

TENT

The miniaturization of camping equipment is a boon to bike hikers. One- or two-man tents are now available in extremely small packages. Tube tents provide a covering against the night air and morning dew while at the same time they can be tightly rolled for easy carrying on your bike. They are fairly expensive, but, like all quality equipment, the more you pay the less you get—in weight and bulk.

One good two-man tent is the Eureka Mt. Marcy that sells for about $40. It's made of rip-stop nylon and gives you a complete floor, side, and top, sewn-together shelter measuring five by eight feet. It's three and a half feet high at the center. The tent weighs four pounds thirteen ounces. Some tents weigh even less, such as Gerry's Pioneer one-man tent at one pound nine ounces.

STOVE

Cooking food over a campfire is feasible and enjoyable if you have the time and expertise to do a good job. However, most bike campers use a small Primus or Svea white-gas stove. Designed originally for high-altitude mountain climbers who require only the smallest and most efficient gear, these stoves are ideal for quick cooking and compactness. Some are designed with compressed gas in a container that is plugged into the stove itself and burns about three hours. Others require that you fill the stove first from a separate container of white gas. Both stoves produce quick hot heat and can boil a small pan of water in a minute and heat soup, chili, or whatever before you can say, "L'Escoffier."

MONEY

Any trip costs money. Bike campers usually compute too low a figure. Two dollars a day for food is not enough, especially when good, healthy food, and plenty of it, is your fuel for the road. Four dollars a person per day is more adequate. Add an extra dollar a day in a cumulative fund for emergencies. You may have to pay a small fee for some of the campgrounds as well as buy a new tire that might be ripped somehow. American Youth Hostels charge a small fee, too.

Those biking by way of motels and coffee shops require more money. Nowadays, motels average about $7–$12 for a single person, $10–$14 for two. Meals prepared for you in a restaurant or coffee shop cost more, too. Depending on your choice, meals could run an average of $6–$10 a day. Be prepared.

Spreading your money resources into cash, travelers checks, and charge cards broadens your base of security. It leaves more time for you to enjoy the trip and not worry about financial disaster.

FOOD

Eat five or six small meals throughout the day, not the usual three big ones. The more food you eat at one sitting the longer it takes to digest it. Never ride at full speed immediately after eating a full meal or you'll likely develop pains in your side.

Dehydrated food, though very expensive, is lightweight and easy to prepare for bike campers. Campers can also buy food at a store immediately before they stop for the day at a campground. That way they won't have to carry the packages all day on their bikes.

Whatever the method, food intake should be judged for each individual by the norm, set by the National Academy of Sciences in 1964, that an average man requires about 2,900 calories of energy to move through an ordinary day. Studies show that bikers, because of the continuous extraordinary energy output they produce during their ordinary day, can burn up to 6,000 calories a day. The average biker uses 660 calories an hour traveling at thirteen miles per hour.

Good food is a must. A judicious mixture of proteins and carbohydrates, and good taste, should be on the menu. I repeat, avoid fried foods and fats. They lard you down like an anchor. Soda pop injects you with quick sugar energy but the carbonation bloats your stomach and diminishes your vitality. Drink soda sparingly. Malts are good all-around drinks. They are energy-packed, satisfy thirst, and are loaded with carbohydrates, the principal source of muscular energy. Honey, or "organic speed," packs an energy wallop, too. Six or seven ounces through the day zings you to life.

GORP

This favorite snack of mountain hikers is good for bicycle hikers as well. Gorp is a mixture of one third peanuts, one third raisins, one third chocolate bits.

Bikers down a handful of gorp as they ride and provide themselves with a high energy-packed, delicious, inexpensive food. Gorp can be carried in a heavy plastic bag. A four-ounce can of peanuts, a six-pack package of raisins, and a six-ounce bag of chocolate chips makes the recipe. The one drawback is that the peanuts and chocolate are thirst-producing. Keep your water jugs full when eating this ambrosia.

FRUIT

The easiest fruits to eat on the road are the ones that need no peeling, such as apples, peaches, grapes, apricots, figs, dates, plums, pears. Vegetables such as tomatoes, celery, carrots, radishes fall into the same category. All that these need is washing. For over-all best results of fruit and vegetable eating, choose the ones with the most moisture, such as the peaches and tomatoes. That way you can satisfy both your thirst and hunger as much as possible.

PACKING THE BIKE

The fundamental rule for packing your bike with supplies is to balance the load left and right and front and rear. In other words, pack the left side of your saddlebags, weigh it, and then pack the right side with the same weight load. You can't carry the same weight on the handlebars as you do on the rear wheel. Nevertheless, put some of your heavier items in the front.

Lay out your supplies on the floor before you pack. Anticipate the items you'll use more frequently than others. Then put those more-used items in the pockets or compartments that are more accessible. For example, your air-pressure gauge should go in the handlebar bag, as should the suntan lotion, the maps, the first-aid kit, your tools. These are items you could use at any time during the day. However, the spare parts, the change of clothes, the toilet kit can be packed deep in the saddlebags.

Once your saddlebags and handlebar bags are packed, keep the contents in the same place throughout the trip. Remember from where you remove the toothbrush kit; return it to the same spot. Replace the bag of gorp in the same place. Pack your bike well the first time and keep it that way on the road.

The time you take to think ahead and pack your bike with care is inversely proportional to how little bother you have with your supplies on the highway. One sign of a good outdoor camper is his thoughtful planning, which shows itself in a simple, well-ordered, clean campsite. The same can be said of a bike hiker. If his bike is packed thoughtfully, it's a sign that he plans to have more time for an enjoyable and memorable trip.

4

MAPPING YOUR ROUTE

The purest bikers among us feel that planning in any degree automatically eliminates the spontaneity of cycling. These are the ones who more often than not find that such spontaneity runs them into industrial sections crowded with trucks and noise or up a road they thought shouldn't have taken them so far out of the way.

Even if your plans are to ramble to your destination, some minimal pre-pedaling planning should be outlined. Knowing where to go and choosing the most interesting route enhances the outing, not detracts from it. Spontaneity doesn't come from total ignorance of your destination and the by-ways to get there. Spontaneity comes with reacting to the scenes surrounding you. How well you use your sense of discovery is based largely on your preparation of the trip and the limitations you set for yourself.

Maps help. The feeling of the carefree open road at fifteen miles per hour can still be with you with maps in your back pocket.

WHAT MAPS ARE

Maps are the abstract outline of a territory or subject, a representation of a section of the earth. The information conveyed is in graphic form, not in words. As a result, you must interpret maps with as much accurate imagination as you can put into the lines and symbols that are used to describe a city or state.

Generally, the information on maps is limited so that its appearance is not cluttered with too much print. Maps are not photographs. They do not include all the details of the territory you are planning to travel through, but for bikers they do contain far more valuable information than is first expected.

Maps indicate everything from air currents to ocean floors, to agricultural areas, to forests, to populations, to river systems, to the surface of the moon. Some states, such as Illinois, publish scenic tour maps that plot out the mileage, sights, and highways of a trip. Usually, the routes are plotted for about 200–300-mile loops to begin and end in the same place. Although the maps are designed for motorists, bikers can use them effectively, too. These scenic tour maps are normally available from a state division of tourism.

Bikers are concerned primarily with road maps, though maps of the terrain, or topological maps ("topo" maps), play an important role also. A few minutes study of a good map can reap many dividends on the road.

ROAD MAPS

Road maps are the easiest basic route-planning tool for bikers. These maps are designed for drivers of cars and trucks, but bikers, having equal right to nearly all the public roads, are included.

Reading a map for bicycling demands more attention than is ordinarily paid to the symbols. Always interpret a map in relation to the legend. The legend is usually located in one of the corners of the map and includes the meaning of all the symbols used on the map. These symbols can provide bikers with much time-saving information.

For example, the official map of Pennsylvania prepared by the Department of Transportation in cooperation with the Department of Environmental Resources of the Pennsylvania

Game Commission has a wide range of information that includes:

State forest land
State game land
State game farms
State or national forest
  picnic areas
Tourist information centers
Hiking trails
Toll roads
Divided highways (access
  partially controlled)
Partial traffic interchanges
Undivided highways (three
  or more lanes)
Unpaved highways
Interstate route numbers
Airports
U.S. highways route num-
  bers
Bordering state route
  numbers

State fish hatcheries
State parks
State forest natural areas
State historical properties
Roadside rests
Points of interest
Interstate highways
Divided highways (access
  fully controlled)
Full traffic interchanges
Divided highways
Two-lane paved highways
Single-lane paved highways
Major highway construction
Interstate route numbers
  (business-area loops)
State route numbers
The state capital

Nine different symbols indicating the varying populations of
  towns and cities.
Mileage between towns and road junctions.
Accumulated mileage between points on highways.

All this information brings a map alive and provides bikers
with valuable reference points, if not destinations. Always
take time to look at a map with these symbols in mind. Every
mark on a map means something specific. Even the size of the
print for names of towns and cities indicates the size of the
population, a help to bikers considering whether they would
prefer to avoid or visit a certain town. The colors on a map
also have specific meanings. The red, green, or black of highways refers to the size of the roads, which in turn often indicates the extent of traffic. The wide, irregular splotches of
colors on maps are not for decoration. They indicate state or

national parks, timberland, rivers, ponds, and lakes, all of interest to bike hikers.

Two other parts of a map are important. The first is the scale of mileage that is usually in or next to the legend of symbols. The scale varies according to each map, but it always gives the number of miles per inch. Mileage, as all bikers know, is important information for any trip. In addition, maps always include a compass printed somewhere on the face, usually in a corner. This is valuable for bikers in knowing not only the lay of the land but also in anticipating wind direction.

On the reverse side of most state maps, additional information is printed that may be of value to bikers. Usually, small insert maps of the major cities are included. Also, a mileage chart of the distances between the major cities by way of state and U.S. highways is usually printed. Check every section of a map for facts and figures that may come in handy on the road or even help you decide on your destination.

The Pennsylvania map, for example, includes the exact location of seventy-five state parks, forty-four state forest and picnic areas, thirteen sites in the Allegheny National Forest, ten historical parks, nine state forest natural areas, and thirty-six historical properties. Besides that, at nearly all of these sites information is given about the availability of swimming, boating, camping, fishing, picnicking, and skiing. This information is useful for both one-day bikers and long-distance two-wheeling tourists.

INTERPRETING A MAP

You can deduce many unprinted bits of information from a map. For example, the symbols for camping sites in state and national parks nearly always mean that wooded areas line the roads up and down both sides of the sites. Streams are usually nearby, too. Many times bikers can expect hills on a road that leads to or by a camping site. Many times, too, a small general store is located near such a site. All this is not printed on a map. It must be inferred.

On a map, country roads that are indicated by slightly wavy lines usually mean very hilly, winding roads in reality. Pay attention to these slight curves of the black-line highways on state maps. They may indicate much harder riding than is first anticipated.

On maps look for the boulevards that connect with U.S. and interstate highways. These roads usually are heavily traveled by cars and trucks turning on and off from the major highways. The traffic increases the closer you get to the cores of the cities.

On maps that indicate skiing areas, you know for certain that roads leading to and from those sites are hilly. Unless you plan to ride specifically to these areas, choose another route for easier riding.

Reservoirs indicate that hilly roads are nearby. So do mountain peaks. Pay attention to the elevation figures of mountains listed on maps. They can give the general difficulty of the roads you may have to climb.

Maps that show scenic roads tell you that bike riding those highways may be quite difficult. Scenic highways usually follow ridge tops of mountains. They are usually constructed to allow for leisurely driving, which means that the twists, turns, and hills of the natural setting are left in the highways as much as possible. Unless you are biking specifically to such a road, avoid it.

BEWARE OF BROCHURES

Many tourist attractions and real estate corporations publish brochures with maps to show the easiest routes to businesses. These brochure maps are not reliable as guides to the area. The brochures are merely promotional come-ons that have little relationship to reality.

The maps on these brochures are usually distorted to make the attractions appear closer to the major centers of population. They provide little detail of the terrain you bike through and give little indication of nearby sites and towns. They are designed to entice, not to inform. Their pictures may be outstanding, but their maps are usually totally inaccurate. Nor-

mally, you never find a mileage scale on promotional maps.
Never use a brochure map to plan a bike trip.

"TOPO" MAPS

In 1882 the United States Geological Survey began its continuing project of producing contour maps of the nation.
Many of the less populated areas are still unmapped, but most
of the major states and cities are. The USGS quadrangle
maps can be valuable for bike hikers.

Topological maps include: seas, lakes, rivers, canals,
swamps, and other bodies of water; mountains, hills, valleys,
and other features of the land surface; towns, cities, roads,
railroads, and boundaries. All these features are useful to
bikers.

The advantage of topo maps over standard road maps is
the relief indications of the land. A contour line on a topo
map represents an imaginary line along a section of earth.
Every part of that line is the same altitude above sea level. On
most topo maps the lines are drawn at twenty-foot intervals.
Elevation numbers are printed at strategic points on the
maps. As a result, the contour lines on a topo map indicate
the degree of slope of hills, mountains, and valleys as well as
their altitude. Lines spaced far apart show a grade that is
shallow. Lines crowded together indicate a steep slope. Lines
that mesh together into one thick solid dark line indicate
cliffs.

The benefits of these maps to bikers are obvious. In planning trips you can judge the difficulty of hills by the number
of lines a road crosses and the elevation figures printed
close-by. You can judge accurately how long a hill climb is
as well as the distance a downhill run is on the other side.
You can plan routes with detailed information not found on
other maps.

The scale of topo maps varies according to the terrain sur-
veyed. Many of them are set to $1 = 62,000$, or one unit of the
map equals 62,000 units on the ground. This comes out to
one inch equaling nearly one mile of the mapped country.
Each map is scaled to miles, feet, and kilometers.

The reverse side of the old series of USGS maps included the standard symbols to be found on the maps proper. The new series does not. However, a folder is available on request when you order the topo maps from the U. S. Geological Survey in Washington, D.C. On these maps are located cities, villages, roads, buildings, ruins, cliff dwellings, trails, railroads, tunnels, power transmission lines, wharves, bridges, ferries, dams, canal locks, reservation lines, land-grant lines, cemeteries, bench marks, oil and gas wells, mines, lighthouses, wells, marshes, aqueducts, sand dunes, mining debris, and many other features of interest to bikers.

WHERE TO GET MAPS

Maps are readily available for the asking. They are used by those distributing them as a means of circulating information about their special interests and providing a service to the public.

Road maps published by gas and oil companies and distributed through their service stations are the most accessible. Generally, the gas-station maps are good for bikers. They give basic information that travelers on the open road need. However, many service-station maps do not include railroad lines, which are sometimes handy reference points for bikers. The service-station maps also may be slightly out of date. New roads are constantly being constructed and old ones being replaced. Get the latest information possible for a long-distance trip. Always check the date of publication on these and other maps. This is difficult at times since many publishers hide dates in obscure parts of the map or put the date in code.

Automobile clubs publish good maps. You must be a member of the club to qualify for its maps. If you're not, find a relative or friend who is and have him request maps for you. On long trips an auto club official can chart a route for you. I requested such a route across country to see what the club would come up with. Beware of automobile club routes for bicycles. The route given me for a bike would have taken me through the center of the Ozark Mountains, the most difficult

country of the South, and across the hottest, most desolate
parts of the southwest desert. Some roads suggested in the
desert were not paved. Besides that, the auto club route was,
I calculated, 550 miles longer than the one I had plotted. I
like to think that the auto club man who designed the route
knew nothing of bike hiking rather than that he felt threatened by the rising tide of the bike culture.

Still, the auto club does provide good maps. If you plan to
cross a few states, having maps that are published by the same
company means that you have the same symbols and format
throughout your trip.

State maps are very good. They include the latest construction projects, are accurate, and usually provide more side information about an area than other maps. They are labeled
"official" and are normally published every year. You can
receive these maps free of charge usually by writing the state
Chamber of Commerce or the Department of Transportation
in the state capital.

City Chambers of Commerce usually publish maps. These,
too, include side information such as local points of interest,
camp sites, motel accommodations, galleries, museums, town
histories, major businesses or industries, and the like. These
maps give details that may be of special help if you are a
stranger to the area.

The USGS topological maps cost $.25 per sheet. They are
labeled according to the major city or county within the
quadrangle of the map and should be ordered as such. The
topo maps can be ordered by writing the U. S. Geological
Survey, General Services Building, 18th and F Streets NW,
Washington, D.C. 20242.

These topo maps are good to have for local riding, but they
can add up to quite an expense if you want to map a complete
long-distance trip. Some bikers order topo maps for areas they
are unfamiliar with or for destinations they know to be hilly
and mountainous. That way they can choose the best route
once they arrive at the steep sections of the trip.

The larger city libraries have map collections that include
road maps as well as contour maps. Some libraries circulate
the maps, some don't. In either case, they provide another

source for specialized maps. The smaller libraries usually have road atlases of each state in the Union. Sometimes even topological atlases like the National Atlas of the United States of America published by the U. S. Department of the Interior are available and are good for planning long trips.

MAPPING A CITY ROUTE

Study city maps for street patterns that lead to the civic center. A bird's-eye view gives you an idea of how the traffic flow moves into and out of town. If the major boulevards are close together, you know that the bulk of cars and trucks concentrates here. If the city lies beside a bay, ocean, lake, or is on a peninsula, you know that most traffic uses the inland side. Bridges of a town next to a body of water are usually crowded all the time, but especially during the rush hours.

If the streets on a map appear narrow, short, and at many angles to each other, you have a city difficult to travel through unless you are familiar with it. If you are a stranger to such a tangled mass of streets, plot your course for the outskirts of town.

Pay special attention to the map symbols. Nearly all city maps show where the schools are located. As a result, you may wish to plan your route so that you avoid the morning and afternoon rush of children, high schoolers, or collegians.

Most city maps indicate the freeways and throughways in colored or heavy black lines. Avoid these, as the law states you must, but avoid the main intersections and turnoffs of the freeways, too. Traffic tends to coagulate around the four-lane, high-speed thoroughfares.

Downtown government centers, business districts, and central shopping areas are always more crowded than other sections of town. Crowds bring cars with them. Avoid these centers unless they are your specific destinations. They are usually symbolized on city maps, or at least you can deduce where they are located by the pattern of streets in the city center.

Roads that follow the edge of a river are usually well traveled and crowded. Sometimes these roads can be good if wide shoulders are available. Otherwise, ride a nearby street at traffic time.

In general, try to pick streets that parallel the main boulevards. City maps show where the parks are. Pick roads that travel by these parks as well as roads that pass college complexes where trees, grass, and flowers usually grow. Often turnpikes and toll roads that lead into or through a city have roads older, narrower, and little used nearby. Check a map and pick these older roads to ride. They are the ones the rush of the modern world has by-passed but are usually just right for bikers.

MAPPING A COUNTRY ROUTE

No matter how long a bike hike into the country you plan, take time beforehand to look at a map larger than the area you're going to cover. That way you can gain a perspective of the country surrounding your proposed route and destination.

This is useful in several ways. First, you can tell in which direction the small creeks and rivers flow next to the roads you may take. Streams usually flow down into rivers. Knowing in which direction the streams flow gives you information about whether the roads that follow the streams go up or downhill in relation to the direction you're heading.

A large-area map also shows you the pattern of roads and highways that surround the route you're planning. If you see a rather large city with only one main highway leading from it, you know that road is used heavily by trucks. It's a road to avoid.

Knowing the pattern of roads also indicates which ones pass through the state and national parks. You may want to extend your trip through one of these beautiful parks, a decision you couldn't make without a map.

Look for the symbols for ski areas and mountain peaks. They invariably indicate hard riding. It is difficult to determine the extent of mountainous regions on a one-dimensional road map. Still, by noticing the areas that are labeled "Ranges" or "Mountains," you can anticipate hard riding. Be careful not to miss these labels. Often you can pay so much attention to the small print on maps that you miss seeing the larger letters spaced across three or four or more inches. Names of mountain ranges are usually printed this way.

On your map go over every inch of the roads you plan to take. Don't simply mark your starting point and your destination and casually look across the gap between them. Follow the highway lines carefully all the way. In doing so you may find a short cut, or a road that has more historical spots, picnic areas, or scenic views along the way. More important, you may find that some roads are not paved. In the midwest farm country and the western deserts especially, many roads are kept in the gravel state either because the minimal traffic doesn't justify the expense of laying asphalt or because the local people prefer the dirt roads. Either way, you have a better trip if you are prepared for such roads.

Some bikers deliberately choose to ride over unpaved roads. They like the pure natural setting and the challenge of slow, deliberate riding that these roads offer, not to mention the unspoiled country they lead to. Nevertheless, the chances of tire punctures and dust and dirt clogging the lubricated parts of your bike increase algebraically. Beginning bike hikers should avoid the unpaved roads.

Once you have plotted your route on a map, take a felt pen and trace the roads you selected. A green or yellow ink stands out the best on a map while at the same time allowing you to see the original printed highways beneath the ink. The tracings make your route easy to see when you come to an intersection and need to refer to the map for the right road to take. Before long you'll see that maps become an integral part of any enjoyable trip.

5

CITY RIDING

The challenge of bicycle riding in Boston, Los Angeles, or any other city is not based on man against nature or man against himself. It's based on man against man.

Bike riders must be extracautious in urban traffic. Perhaps because city riding is indeed more likely to produce broken bones and bikes, city bikers are therefore more alert to such possibilities than country bikers. Even though 73.5 per cent of the national population lives in cities, the number of bicycle deaths resulting in collisions is about equal in city and rural areas—450 deaths in cities, 400 in rural sections. Bicycle drivers must share the responsibilities of the road with car drivers.

VEHICLE CODES

All vehicles that share the public roadways are subject to the laws of the state. That includes bicycles in the city as well as in the country. As a result, bikers must realize that, being subject to the rights and responsibilities of operating a vehicle, they are liable to traffic tickets and prosecution just as are drivers of automobiles, trucks, and motorcycles. Most bikers are not aware of this, or at least don't ride with this in mind. Remember that, like car drivers, bicyclists are liable to arrest and prosecution in hit-and-run cases involving either pedestrians or parked cars.

The Illinois Rules of the Road, for example, state that, "Persons riding bicycles or animals, or driving animal-drawn vehicles, must observe the traffic laws, as well as pedestrians and drivers of motor vehicles; and it is a misdemeanor for any person to disregard the law or to fail to do something required thereby. Penalties include fines ranging from ten to 500 dollars and/or imprisonment from ten days to six months."

Prior to the boom in bike riding, most state vehicle codes as they applied to bicycles were not vigorously enforced. However, now that millions of bike riders are mixing with car drivers on the highways and city roads, more local police departments are stopping more bike riders to issue warnings and tickets for violations of traffic regulations.

Arcadia, California, is one town that, faced with increased bicycle traffic and accidents, suddenly began a campaign for safer, more law-abiding riding. In the first week of its police department campaign, more than 100 local bike riders were issued citations for breaking the law. The citations, most of them warnings at first, were issued to both children and adults. The majority of the citations were for riding on the wrong side of the street, running stop signs, and riding two to a bike. The word spread quickly through town that the maverick bike-riding days were over.

The laws of California, our most populous state, include the basic laws that apply to bicycles in the other states. They deserve repeating here:

California Vehicle Code Sections Relating to Bicycles

Laws Applicable to Bicycle Use

21200.   Every person riding a bicycle upon a roadway has all the rights and is subject to all the duties applicable to the driver of a vehicle except those provisions which by their very nature can have no applications.

Equipment Requirements

21201. (a) No person shall operate a bicycle on a roadway unless it is equipped with a brake which will enable the operator to make one braked wheel skid on dry, level, clean pavement.

(b) No person shall operate on the highway any bicycle equipped with handlebars so raised that the operator must elevate his hands above the level of his shoulders in order to grasp the normal steering grip area.

(c) No person shall operate upon any highway a bicycle which has been modified or altered in such a way as to cause the pedal in its lowermost position to be more than twelve inches above the ground.

(d) Every bicycle operated upon any highway during darkness shall be equipped with a lamp emitting a white light visible from a distance of 300 feet in front of the bicycle and with a red reflector on the rear of a type approved by the department which shall be visible from a distance of 300 feet to the rear when directly in front of lawful upper beams of headlamps on a motor vehicle. A lamp emitting a red light visible from 300 feet to the rear may be used in addition to the red reflector.

Keep to Right

21202. Every person operating a bicycle upon a roadway shall ride as near to the right side of the roadway as practicable, exercising due care when passing a standing vehicle or one proceeding in the same direction.

Hitching Rides

21203. No person riding upon any bicycle, coaster, roller skates, sled or toy vehicle shall attach the same or himself to any streetcar or vehicle on the roadway.

Riding on Bicycles

21204. (a) A person propelling a bicycle shall not ride other than upon or astride a permanent and regular seat attached thereto.

(b) No person operating a bicycle upon a highway shall permit any person to ride on the handlebars.

Carrying Articles

21205. No person operating a bicycle shall carry any package, bundle or article which prevents the operator from keeping at least one hand upon the handlebars.

In addition to the state code, most municipal codes have sections dealing with bicycles. The Arcadia Municipal Code Section 3320 (Business Sidewalk Operation), for example, says, "No person shall use or operate any bicycle or wheeled toy upon any sidewalk in a business district or adjacent to any place of public assembly."

WHAT THE CODES MEAN

Basically, the state and municipal codes, which may vary in detail from state to state and city to city, establish the same broad rules and regulations across the country. First of all, bike riders must always ride *with* the traffic. (Pedestrians walk against the traffic.) Just as for any other vehicle, it is against the law to ride a bicycle against oncoming cars and trucks.

Therefore, bikers must ride on the right-hand side of the road as close to the curb or shoulder of the road as safety permits. Just as must operators of other kinds of vehicles, bicyclists must signal their turns with their left hand. Straight up indicates a right turn. Straight out to the left paralleling the ground indicates a left turn. A forty-five-degree hand signal pointing toward the ground indicates a stop or slowing down.

As with other vehicles, bicycles must have sufficient illumination in both front and rear directions at night. (Some states require lights and reflectors to be visible for 500 feet.) Bicycles, as with other vehicles, must not be ridden on sidewalks. Sidewalks are for walkers. Bikers must obey all traffic lights and traffic signs, including those that stipulate no bicycle riding on certain marked roads such as freeways and parkways.

Bikers must operate their vehicles, as must drivers of cars

and trucks, with the safety that is consistent with the design
of their vehicles. That means bikers must not speed, must not
ride double on one bike (except for tandems, bicycles are not
designed for riding double), nor must they alter their bikes
so that they become ill-designed and therefore unsafe. Rais-
ing the handlebars so that you have to reach high above your
shoulders to steer is an example and a speedy way to the
hospital.

In California the pedestrian has the right of way over the
automobile driver. California is the exception in this country
in this priority. Most of the other states reverse the order:
the driver has the right of way over the pedestrian.

It follows in California then that bicyclists on their vehicles must defer to all pedestrians. However, even though that
may not follow in the other states where the order is re-
versed, it is good sense, good safety, and good manners for
bikers always to defer to pedestrians. At this point in the
twentieth century, we are beginning a changeover to a different style of living. Bicycle riding is part of the new life-style
of good health and communication with the outdoors. If bike
riders establish at the outset that they are considerate on the
road, then perhaps in the future bicyclists will develop a better reputation with those who walk than the reputation car
drivers now have. Give pedestrians the right of way wherever
you live.

One of the important by-products of the state codes that
include sections on bicycles is that drivers of cars, trucks, and
motorcycles must regard you as an equal in terms of your
rights on the highway. The California Driver's Handbook
states explicitly in bold type, "Drivers of motor vehicles must
treat you [bicyclists] as they would another motor vehicle."

That means car drivers must defer to your left and right
turns under the law. They must acknowledge your speed
capabilities and vehicle design. They must give you safe distance from the rear. They must signal for your benefit. They
must pass you on the left with safety and not turn sharply in
front of you after the pass. In short, they must take you into
the scope of the laws of the road. You have as much right
to the road as they do.

SPEED KILLS

Losing control of your bike when you're zooming downhill at forty miles per hour is disastrous. Being hit by a car at forty miles per hour is catastrophic.

In 1971 more than 56,000 people were killed in auto accidents. More than half of those accidents were the result of drunken driving. Some drivers, drunk or not, are downright malicious, and some are merely inept. What bikers must keep in mind is that an automobile is an extremely dangerous weapon when in the hands of either a first-class rat or a buffoon. It doesn't matter which.

Car drivers are encased in a shell of iron that gives them not only real protection when they are bumped slightly by another car but also a false sense of security when they are fantasizing a road race. Because of this, car drivers, feeling that their bunker of steel protects them, take unnecessary chances on the road. Too often it's the feeling that keeps the accelerator to the floor.

Bikers, however, have no real protection on their skeletons of steel when they are bumped slightly by a car, nor do they harbor any false sense of security. Indeed, they have no security. As a result of the enormous power inbred in cars and trucks, bicycle riders must pay special attention to all kinds of traffic on the road. They must keep alert for cars and trucks behind them as well as in front of them. They must pay attention to the cars on the far side of the road traveling in the opposite direction. They must anticipate when a car will turn right in front of them. They must ride with the presumption that no car driver sees them. At the same time, they themselves must be aware of all the cars in sight.

The following table of stopping distances for cars is the reason bikers must be watchful. The total distance it takes for a car to stop at various speeds is longer than people realize. Bikers should be aware of these distances so that they can anticipate escape routes in case of impending doom. This stopping distance for a car includes the time it takes for the driver to react from eye to brain to foot to wheel to road.

Car Stopping Distance

(*in feet*)

MPH	THINKING DISTANCE	BRAKING DISTANCE	TOTAL
25	27	34.4	61.4
35	38	67	105
45	49	110	159
55	60	165	225
65	71	231	302

As you can see, the distance it takes to rein in a multi-horsepower behemoth to a stop is unsettling. Bikers, beware. Keep on the lookout for car-driving deviates, even at low speeds. Think ahead. Always have a plan of action to avoid possible accidents that may occur in the next few seconds. Watch for alternate routes to swerve away from skidding cars. Safeguards are better than stretchers.

Here's the clincher. National Safety Council studies indicate that approximately 80 per cent of the deaths of bike riders hit by automobiles resulted entirely from the fault of the bikers, not the car drivers. The total number of bicycling deaths from all causes is up 73 per cent from 1961. The death figure has climbed steadily, though fortunately well below the increase in the number of riders. The deaths of bicyclists in the last few years were:

1972	—	1,000
1971	—	850
1970	—	820
1969	—	800
1968	—	790
1967	—	750

Of the 850 deaths in 1971, 500 were youngsters in the five–fourteen-year-old group, 200 in the fifteen–twenty-four-year-old group, and the rest spread among the other ages.

The other nearly 40,000 bicyclists injured each year might

have avoided accidents if they, too, had been more cautious. A survey by the Bicycle Institute of America shows that 88 per cent of all accidents involving bikers happened in residential areas during the day and in clear weather.

BIKEWAYS

To minimize accidents in city traffic, many city councils are passing proposals to establish routes for bike riding in their towns. The city traffic and engineering departments plan the routes. The routes are usually a result of pressure from bicycle clubs or unorganized bands of bikers wanting some recognition and accommodations to be given them by the city. The phenomenal increase in bike riding in recent years forces many cities to take into account safety and enjoyment for the bicyclists.

For example, eighteen cities in the San Gabriel Valley, California, are studying ways and means of joining together in one over-all plan. Some states have plans to connect their bikeways with neighboring states. The hope is that bike routes eventually will be established throughout the country so that bikers can ride from coast to coast and border to border on interconnecting trails.

Bikeways are divided into three general types—bike routes, bike lanes, bike paths. All have been helpful in reducing the number of accidents and traffic citations. Cities that do plan or construct bikeways meet a definite need of the residents and provide a base for future planning and development.

Davis, California, is a prime example. One set of figures shows the growing education of bike riders who responded to city planning and involvement. In 1966 bikers in Davis were issued 1,250 tickets for not stopping at stop signs and stoplights, riding on the wrong side of the street, riding double, riding on the sidewalk, and parking in unsafe and unauthorized places. During this time bikeways in Davis were being developed. The following year the number of citations was reduced to 765. Only 590 citations were issued in 1968, 597 in 1969, and 311 in 1970. It would be difficult to establish a direct cause-and-effect relationship between bikeways and safer riding, but the indications are certainly clear.

BIKE ROUTES

Generally, bike routes are the simplest form of bike planning. The routes used are marked by a traffic sign with the picture of a bike and an arrow pointing in the direction bikers can follow. The routes planned by the city traffic engineers generally take the way of least resistance through residential areas, on streets that parallel main arteries, and often make loops back to a starting place. The engineers plan the routes so that most of the turns are right-hand. That way bikers do not have to make left-hand turns from the center lanes.

Arcadia, California, has four bikeway loops totaling thirty-five miles. The routes are posted with directional signs and are designed so that the few left-hand turns on them occur primarily at boulevard stop signs or signals.

The Indiana Division of Tourism distributes on request about thirty-five bike routes. The maps cover all sections of the state, including twenty-five-mile loops through major cities as well as ninety-mile trips through the countryside.

Unfortunately, most of the bike routes in cities and states around the country are little more than token recognition by city councils to quiet the bikers' uproar. Basically, the routes are political appeasements that do little to attack the real problems of increasing bicycle traffic on the streets. They are better than nothing and are a first step, but a few signs and arrows do not eliminate bicycle and automobile hazards in the downtown areas.

BIKE LANES

The second level of development is the bike lane. A lane of traffic is set aside for the exclusive use of bicycles. Most often, the parking lane on one side of the street is usurped from the car driver and given the bicyclist, not without cries of outrage and indignation. The car driver has grown to expect exclusive right to public roads, which is totally out of proportion to both reality and the law.

The bike traffic lane algebraically reduces the likelihood of accidents. Riders can pedal along without worry of a car sideswiping them, stopping suddenly in front of them, or turning sharply without warning into a driveway or cross street.

At this point few towns can justify a full-fledged bike lane in downtown areas. The biking population in most towns is not large enough yet to warrant a separate twenty-four-hour lane of its own while the car traffic continues to be congested.

However, one alternative to taking over a car-parking lane for exclusive bike riding is to establish a limited-access lane. In other words, a parking lane is cleared at certain times of the day so that bicyclists ride in safety during those times. Arcadia, California, is considering this idea for elementary and secondary school students. Certain streets that lead to neighborhood schools would have the parking lane on the right-hand side closed to cars and open to bike riders in the morning. Then after school the other side of the street would be closed to parked cars and open to bike riders going home. This way the parking lane could be used by cars during the hours when school was in session, early in the morning, and late at night. Sharing a lane is a sensible idea.

On a more permanent scale, the construction of a curblike concrete barrier between the bike lane and car lane is being experimented with in several cities. In Davis, where 23,000 bicycles are registered for the 28,000 population (a campus of the University of California is located there), a bike lane separated by concrete is feasible.

In most plans such a lane requires eight feet of parking, six feet of bike lane, and eleven feet of travel lane. This totals twenty-five feet for one half of the road, the standard width for one half of most American city streets. The construction of such a bike lane with barriers to keep cars out of the way runs to about $1,250 per mile for labor, materials, equipment.

In a town such as Davis, passage of funds for this type of bike lane is possible. On Third Street in downtown Davis, bicycle traffic accounts for at least 40 per cent of the total. In addition, 90 per cent of those riding bikes are adults. However, in most towns, the figures are much lower and in reality do not yet justify the space or the funds. The future will be different.

BIKE PATHS

The third level of development is the construction of bike paths. These are usually built for the exclusive use of bikers, though they are open for walkers, too. Most of the bike paths are routed through scenic areas such as parkways, open fields, along riversides, and the like.

Bike paths are the direct result of enlightened city planning. Usually, bicycle clubs have presented their cases to city councils with the emphasis that bike paths are, ultimately, for the benefit of the city as a whole. Everyone in town does not have to own a bicycle in order for the town to be justified in building a bike path, just as everyone does not need to have his house burn down in order to justify a tax-supported fire station.

For motorists and bikers alike, bike paths are the safest routes to travel. No cars are allowed (or are, in fact, capable of fitting the paths), nor are motorcycles or any other motor vehicles. The grades are nearly level, and rest stops with water, benches, and toilet facilities are usually spaced frequently.

More big cities are incorporating bike paths into their plans for urban renewal. In Wichita, Kansas (population 276,554), a three-mile bike path was built as part of its redevelopment plan. The bike path is a strip of asphalt three feet wide that follows the Arkansas River running through the city. The banks of the river are green with grass in summer. Trees are newly planted. Benches are spaced strategically along the way. The new library building is nearby. What formerly was a scar of sand bogs and run-down buildings is now an attractive parkway that bicyclists and walkers can enjoy without the hassle of cars and noise. In addition, the bike path makes a pleasant panorama of the river and city and dresses up what previously had been a Raggedy Anne part of town.

Lincoln, Massachusetts (population 7,567), is another

town that constructed its own bike paths. This small town, an oasis in the middle of the Boston suburban sprawl, built a four-mile bike path that parallels the main street of town. The path winds among trees and mansions, parks and public library, apple orchards and wild land. It is a boon to bikers.

Other big cities and small towns around the country are striking chords for the good life. Robert Cleckner, field director of the Bicycle Institute of America, reports one of the more unusual but perfectly logical methods of some of the progressive community directors. Several cities have already bought the rights of way to abandoned railroads and converted them into bike paths. Many such projects are currently under discussion and negotiation.

One project is the transformation of a six-mile-long railroad bed into a bike path through the Shimek Forest near Burlington, Iowa. Fred Preiwert, director of the Iowa Conservation Commission, gained title to the land. In Ohio, Summit County Director John Daily gained a lease on the thirty-mile right of way on the abandoned Penn Central railroad line from Akron to Cleveland. As a result, a biker can ride to Cleveland or Akron through beautiful rolling country without the danger of automobiles at his back.

The same type of energy was focused in Illinois. Gunnar Peterson, director for Open Lands Project, joined forces with the Illinois Prairie Path Association to transform thirty-one miles of the abandoned Chicago Aurora and Elgin railroad line into a combination biking, hiking, and nature trail. The path is now so well developed and beautiful that it is officially a National Trail.

The more bike paths are developed in the outlying areas the more likely that everyone will see their benefit. Once this happens, the battle to develop bike paths in cities, where they are needed most, will be easier.

BIKING WITHOUT BIKEWAYS

As it is now, most cities do not have bikeways, and the ones that do have had them too short a time to test and evaluate their effectiveness. That means bikers must continue to contend with city traffic and nonplanning. However, with a few conscientiously applied rules, bikers can find city traveling less perilous than it appears.

First of all, avoid the main streets. If possible, and it usually is, ride on a side street that parallels the one with heavy traffic. You're riding a bicycle. That's the first step in acknowledging that you don't have to be part of the crowd. Besides, you get to your destination quicker and in better spirits on an easy-flowing side street.

Maintain a steady course as you ride. Other bikers and car drivers must feel secure in the knowledge that you'll continue ahead competently. If you have trouble steering straight, practice on an empty street by riding the middle line. Keep your front wheel on the white line. Practice until you're almost perfect. Then ride off the line and *pretend* that you are following a white line. Steering a straight course is an acquired habit that can be gained by anyone.

Don't panic at loud noises. Cities are noisy and so are the people in them. Keep your bike as steady and straight as possible when a car suddenly blares its horn at you. Maintain your equilibrium at the loud barking of a dog at your heels. Remain calm at the banging of a truck door or the blowing of a train whistle or the roar of a landing jet overhead. These and other loud noises can frighten you so much that you swerve to avoid them and what they represent. That swerving turns you into oncoming cars and trucks or takes your attention away from your line of direction. Either puts you in danger of an accident.

BIKES AND CARS

Riding among cars in the city demands constant alertness. Ride in traffic only if you must, and then be sure to ride in a straight line with traffic, not against it: riding with the flow of cars reduces the force of impact in case of an accident. Bear in mind that serious accidents can happen even when both you and a car driver are poking along at slow speed.

For bikers, intersections are the most dangerous riding

areas on city streets. You must watch myriad possibilities for mishaps, including signals, turning drivers, pedestrians, parked cars, opening doors, other bikers. Approach an intersection with caution and easy pedaling. Keep your hands on your brakes.

Ride only on streets that allow car parking. These streets have space near the curb for you to ride away from moving traffic. If you must ride between a lane of parked cars and a lane of stopped or slow-moving traffic, do so with eyes open to both sides of you. With hands on brakes, ride slowly down such a corridor. Beware of a driver in a parked car who suddenly opens his door into your lane. Look ahead through the back window of these parked cars to see if the driver's seat is occupied. At the same time, check the drivers of cars in the travel lane on your left. Notice any indication whatsoever that they may turn right into your narrow lane without seeing you.

If you're riding beside a lane of parked cars with no traffic on your left, ride about three feet away from the parked cars. This way you can avoid a driver suddenly starting his car into your path and prevent a nasty crack-up.

Watch for children darting into the street from between parked cars, especially on residential streets. A ball may roll into the street and a few seconds later a boy or girl may follow it without looking for traffic. Many accidents happen this way.

Stan Swain, a bicycle racer from New England, was involved in just such a situation. For more than ten years Swain had been developing his racing prowess to compete on the American team for the 1972 Olympics in Munich. Being part of the Olympic team was a decade-long goal, the summit of a program of intense daily training, participation in all the races he could enter, and training with possible future members of the Olympic team. One week before he was to try out for the Olympic team, a child ran into the street and Swain swerved, fell down, and broke his wrist. It was impossible for him to compete for the tryouts, a tragic blow. To make matters worse, one of the racers who made the American team was one Swain had beaten many times in other races. Moral:

watch for children running into the streets (even if you're not trying out for the Olympic bicycling team).

At intersections keep your eyes and ears open for cars coming and going in all directions. Defer to pedestrians and cars alike unless it is obvious that you can proceed with absolute safety.

At stoplights ride to the front of the first car at the intersection or pedestrian crosswalk. This way you avoid inhaling the exhausts of any stopped cars in front of you. Then when the signal changes to green, hesitate, look over your shoulder, and be certain that no car in the lane next to you is going to turn right. That turn could end up into you. It's often a good idea to wait until all the cars are on their way past you before you push off and pedal.

Car drivers often cannot judge the speed, let alone the vulnerability, of a bike rider. Many times car drivers have suddenly turned to the right onto a side street and nearly sent me flying through the air in the process. This type of driving usually happens on cross streets where the driver doesn't have to stop for a stop sign or signal. Now I glance over my shoulder when I approach every cross street to see if a driver gives any sign of turning. If he does, I slow down and give him the right of way.

Remember that car drivers as a whole are rather immune to the reality of accidents. In this country few motorists stop at the scene of an accident. If they do, it's to gawk rather than to help. If an accident happens during rush hours when everyone's unshakable goal is to get home in the fastest time possible, the accident and those involved in it, it appears, are undeserving of any kind of sympathy.

Once, in Erie, Pennsylvania, I made the mistake of riding through town during the 4:30 P.M. retreat from work. At one crowded intersection I signaled for a left turn and eased into the proper lane. At the cross street a driver saw me coming, but apparently I was merely a bicycle rider who warranted no space on the road with the big boys. The driver bucked the stop sign. We eyed each other as we moved irretrievably toward the same lane. My mistake was to assume that the driver understood that I had the right of way as well as realizing that an automobile is incalculably more deadly than a bicycle. I continued on course while all the time I grew more enraged at the stop-sign jumper who by now was commander of all tank units of the United States Army. We converged to one foot short of collision point. The Detroit demon cut in front of me. Its rear bumper was at my front wheel. Then I crossed the point of no return. My right foot was inches away from being mangled. I panicked, twisted the bike to get out of the way, lost balance, and fell down. Raisins, suntan lotion, air-pressure gauge, screwdriver, pliers, wrench, and air pump scattered over the street. The front wheel of the bike twisted as it hit the asphalt. A screw on the carrier rack sprang out. I sat in the middle of a circle of grumbling automobiles and watched with fury as the culprit driver casually looked over her shoulder to see if I was alive before she continued down the street. The other drivers watched blank-eyed while I stood up, gathered my gear, and carried my twisted bike to the curb. No one asked whether I was hurt. No one offered any help.

Before you get into a similar situation and temporarily lose faith in your fellow man, stay clear of the traffic hour. When car meets bicycle, the life you save is your own.

BIKES AND TRUCKS

Truck drivers are professional drivers. Their problems with driving in cities are bad enough without bikers adding to them. Bikers are well advised to stay clear of trucks, not only as the ultimate prevention against accidents, but also to keep away from the Goliaths that, this time, win all battles against the Davids on their tiny two-wheelers.

Generally, bikers should take alternate routes when they spot a sign on the side of the road that indicates a truck route. Bikers with saddlebags on their racks and who are geared up for overnight trips place themselves in unnecessary situations with bulky bikes next to trucks. Take the less-traveled streets.

In cities trucks deliver and pick up goods. This means that trucks frequently swing out to the middle of the street and back into receiving docks and storage rooms. Bikers must be exceptionally aware of trucks in the process of backing up. Never ride behind a truck that is in position to back up or, in fact, is backing up. This is disastrous. Truck drivers have limited visibility to guide their huge machines. Always defer to trucks. Always wait until they are parked in place and stopped before you move on.

Some trucks have bells that ring automatically when the drivers shift to reverse. The bells are a warning device. They're more effective than a mirror or horn. Still, some people aren't sure what the bells mean. Know that the loud, fast continual ringing is meant to warn you that a truck nearby is backing up. Watch for it.

On the streets give all trucks wide berth. Pass them only with extreme caution and only when you can see the driver's eyes on you through his side mirror. Never presume that a truck driver sees you unless you actually meet eye to eye.

As with cars, ride your bike in a straight line in truck traffic to show the driver that you know what you're doing and that you will not veer suddenly into the traffic lane. If a trucker blows his big horn at you, remain calm. Try not to jerk your bike spastically in reaction to the loud noise. This sudden movement only increases your chances of mishaps. Keep riding. Glance over your shoulder to see what the problem is. The trucker may be honking at a car or another truck or a wayward pedestrian. He may merely want to warn you that he is passing on your left. He may want you to get closer to the right side of the street so he can pass with safety and not be forced to cross the double line into oncoming traffic. If he wants to pass you, pull over to the side or stop completely. Always let him have the right of way. It's the best way for both of you.

ANALYZE THE CITY

If you plan trips through and within your own city, sit down and carefully consider your routes. You may know your hometown by way of automobile, bus, or subway, but selecting a route for a bicycle takes a different perspective.

The same is true of a city with which you are unfamiliar. Take a map of that city and study it for bike hiking before you set out on your trip. Have a plan of attack on a strange city so that you reduce the chances of being overwhelmed by it once you're there. These are some of the things to look for:

Know where the state and U.S. highways lead into the city. Often a main highway passes through the center of town. If you follow such a route without realizing that a by-pass exists, you've made extra headaches and hassle for yourself. A by-pass frees you from having to ride through heavy downtown traffic. Frequently, if you wish, you can easily avoid the city cores simply by checking a map beforehand.

Know where proposed highways are planned in the city. Maps often show these projects in dotted lines. Areas around these proposed highways are often places to avoid. They automatically mean construction equipment, noise, and congestion, since workers are in the process of either leveling the houses and office buildings in preparation for the new highway or actually laying the concrete.

Know that industrial areas of most towns and cities are on the outskirts of the city limits. Sometimes these areas are situated on one side of the city while the other side is mostly free of the truck traffic that accompanies manufacturing. Know which side of town is which. Remember, too, that Sundays in industrial sections of town are as free from traffic as church parking lots on Wednesdays.

Look at a map to see where the municipal parks are located. Often it is a pleasant route to wind through a town on streets that connect the parks and playgrounds. Nearly all city maps show such parks.

Other pleasant areas to look for are golf courses, fair grounds, idle race tracks, colleges, rest homes, and hospitals. These are usually spaced in the more comfortable settings of the city and provide trees, green grass, and open spaces to ride through and by. Plan your route so that you pedal by these instead of riding helter-skelter and perhaps missing them by one block.

Look for lakes and ponds in the city. Plan your route along

these for fresh air and good sights. Know where the streams and rivers pass through town. Often a road follows a meandering river and provides an interesting bike ride. Bridges can give you views you didn't expect. So can piers and harborways. They are usually all on city maps.

Every city is unique. Understand each one for what it in particular has to offer and where that offering is located. Keep in mind when planning a route that you are riding a bicycle and not driving a car. If the pattern of city streets and highways on a map is laid out in a fan shape, like St. Louis, realize that the closer to the focal point you get the more uncomfortable is the bike riding. If a city is laid out in a somewhat square pattern, like Phoenix, then you can see that it is relatively easy to get around the city core from any side.

Some maps indicate, in addition to the central business sections, where the major truck routes are located. Take advantage of this information and plan how to avoid those areas. On the other hand, if you wish to find a bicycle shop, coffee shop, motel, gas station, Chamber of Commerce, shoeshop, or whatever, the most likely areas would be on the main highways and in the civic-center business areas.

Airports are often good acreage to ride around. Most of the airports are on level ground, have low-level buildings, usually are at least beyond the city limits if not in the country, provide long-range vistas, and give you the feeling of openness. The two principal drawbacks are that airports are noisy at jet takeoff and landing times and fill the nearby streets and highways with heavy traffic during the peak hours of airplane travel.

BEST RIDING TIME

More often than not, bicyclists are forced to ride through a city on a schedule not of their own choosing. They have come to the point in their riding day when they have to stop at the city limits or push through the morning and evening traffic. Bikers, being what they are, push through.

However, if you do have the choice, exercise it with a few hints in mind. Remember that the peak car-traffic hours are normally from seven until nine in the morning. Traffic tapers off during the rest of the morning until shortly before noon. People then drive to business lunches, home for lunch, or to do some shopping during their lunch breaks. This usually lasts until about 1:30. The afternoon traffic tapers off until about four. Then from about four until six o'clock in the evening congestion fills the streets again.

With these hours of peak traffic in mind, bikers should plan their assault on a city when the automobile congestion is at a minimum. Either ride a city at sunrise, at midmorning, at midafternoon, or in the evening if the sun is still lighting the world.

You may be in no hurry and have the opportunity to choose your time of day for city riding. If so, ride after the morning traffic and before noon. These midmorning hours are when motorists and people in general are normally the most alert of any time block during the day. Their energy is high, they are fully awake, and they are moving through their day at optimum briskness. You are then at the safest hours.

On the other hand, car drivers on their way to work in the early morning are still groggy from waking up and the thought of another full day ahead of them. They are not apt to respond vigorously to the safety of bicyclists, to say the least. Motorists in evening traffic present similar hazards. This is the time of day when drivers are tired from work or shopping and want only to survive the rush hour so they can make it home to dinner and television. They are not as alert to the possibilities of mishaps with two-wheel disrupters of the homing instinct.

If possible, ride through a city other than during the morning and evening rush hours. You reduce the likelihood of accidents and enjoy the riding much more. You're out of both the pollution of traffic as well as the irritation, grumpiness, and horn blowing of tired drivers. Besides that, you end up realizing that city riding is not as bad as it seems and can indeed offer you sights, sounds, and smells you never dreamed existed when you were windowed tight in a car. Definitely, city riding can become a positive attraction with some minimal planning and precautions.

6

COUNTRY AND MOUNTAIN RIDING

No other setting is as enjoyable for bike hiking as the country. Fresh air, bright skies, trees, creeks, and birds are all about you. The openness of long roads and the freedom of buildingless horizons combine to make bicycle riding one of the most rejuvenating pleasures you can have.

Unfortunately, there's more to riding the countryside and mountains than fresh air and flat roads. Rain, hills, cliffs, rocks, potholes, and country motorists are some of the obstacles you must guard against. Nothing is perfect.

ONE EYE FOR TREES—ONE EYE FOR TRAFFIC

Car drivers in the country must be watched with special care. The quantity of traffic outside the cities is less. The quality is not far behind. Country drivers are used to relatively traffic-free roads. As a result, they often turn from intersections or tree-hidden forks in the highways without looking. They tend to run stop signs because usually no car has intercepted their line of direction in the last thirty minutes. They tend to straddle the white line, if a white line exists. The habit of being the only car on the road is difficult to shake. Often country drivers resent other moving vehicles, which they consider, in an oblique deduction, annoying competition. All country drivers do not drive this way, but those who do are the ones you must be aware of.

Enjoy the surroundings, but keep a watch out for tractors that head off the farm and onto the road without stopping. The noise of the tractor motor may completely absorb the driver's attention. He may not see you; certainly he won't hear you. Farmers are also known to drive their pickup trucks like their tractors. Watch for any kind of vehicle when you approach a farmhouse area or, for that matter, any semi-sheltered road that leads from a farm field. Always give the driver of a tractor or pickup the right of way.

On roads that are lined with trees, be especially cautious of cars that speed into a cross street. You may hear an oncoming car through the trees, but if you can't see it you can easily misjudge its location, direction, and speed. Slow down at all blind intersections.

Think ahead. As you approach the bottom of any size hill, and the road turns right, stay close to the right side of the road. Cars may gather downhill speed and come barreling around the bend that hides you from them. In other words, watch out for cars both in front of and behind you.

BIKE FLAGS

Many groups of bikers now use bike flags as a safety precaution while riding on the high-speed open roads. These flags are usually highly visible, fluorescent red pennants that can easily be seen from a distance by automobile and truck drivers.

The flag is attached to a six- or seven-foot lightweight pole that is hooked to the rear wheel axle. It attracts a driver's attention and is as effective in city traffic as on the highways. Certainly it is one more device to ensure safe biking.

One such flag can be ordered from Bike Safe, Dept. S, Box 1005, Marion, Indiana 46952, for approximately $3.75.

COUNTRY ROADS—WHAT TO EXPECT

Roads outside the cities are unpredictable. Some are well maintained by the state, others are left to rot in the weather year after year. It is impossible to tell from maps which are which. If you are faced with a choice of two roads in the woods, the best source of information is the local population. Ask gas-station attendants, grocery-store clerks, walkers-by-the-side-of-the-road, old-timers sitting in rocking chairs on front porches, grandfathers at the mailboxes, anyone who can tell you for sure what's ahead.

Most country roads that bikers favor for unharassed riding are not the super roads that get all the attention. This means that bikers should watch for such hazards as potholes and bumps, the acne of backwoods byways. Rain, wear and tear, and lack of proper maintenance erode the asphalt of country routes. If not avoided, these ruts and debris can cause accidents.

Be alert to the downy woodpeckers on the maple trees, but also be alert to the dangers on the roads that take you to the trees. Never ride over potholes filled with water. These are deceiving since water assumes the shape of its container. The holes may be an inch deep or a foot deep, you can't tell which from their appearances. Stay clear of them or they may puncture your tube, bend your rim, and will probably spill you over the handlebars.

Watch for sharp rocks, especially in mountainous areas. The earth is slow-moving, but it is alive. Wind and rain loosen rocks on the sides of cliffs. The rocks fall to the roads. Pointed one-inch pebbles make no mark on an automobile tire, but they can damage bicycle tires. Watch for them.

Along with the rocks that fall to the road come sand and dirt. Sand can be as slippery as wax for a bike. If you spot sand on a curve and you're traveling fast, slow down at once. A slight angle in your riding balance can result in your wheels slipping out from under you. You may end up in a bad fall. Even sand on a flat road can be risky at high speeds. Take it easy. Usually, you can follow car tracks that have swept the sand away and feel secure.

CATTLE GUARDS AND RAILROAD TRACKS

In ranching areas many roads have cattle guards to help control wayward beef. These guards are a series of five-inch pipes that are laid entirely across the road from shoulder to shoulder. Usually, they form a small bridge over a creek or ravine. They take the place of asphalt and are strong enough for car and truck traffic. Their purpose is to keep stray cattle from crossing them in either direction and thereby prevent them from continuing down the highway. Cattle cannot walk over the guards since their hoofs slip into the gaps between the pipes.

Never ride your bike across these cattle guards. They are like potholes. You can damage your bike or take a bad spill or both. Get off and walk your two-wheeler across the bridge. Unfortunately, few cattle guards have signs that warn of their location since cars and trucks have no problem with them. Except for the square A-frame braces of the sides of the guards, from a distance they look like any normal paved bridge over a small stream. If you approach one (they are found more in the West than elsewhere) and suddenly realize what it is, brake immediately to a complete stop or you'll wind up worse than the cattle.

The same is true of railroad tracks. Slow down to absolute minimal speed as you approach a railroad crossing. Even though a crossing appears smooth from asphalt to tracks to asphalt, never ride across one at high speed. An unbending railroad crossing that is unlevel even an inch can bend your rim when you jolt over it. The sharp edge of a railing can rip your tire. It's better to ease over the crossing, best to walk your bike over it. Eliminate the possibility of damage and resulting frustration.

MUTTS, MONGRELS, AND OTHER MONSTERS

Dogs are epidemic in the United States. Man's best friend turns into the biker's worst enemy. They are often more dangerous than a burly trucker who hates two-wheeling freaks monopolizing the public roadways. In short, dogs are the bane of the bicycling world.

Unfortunately, no one has unraveled satisfactorily the mystery of why most dogs become enraged at passing bikers. The bikers don't know and neither do the veterinarians. Theories abound. One is that the spinning spokes of a bicycle create a sound pitch above the human hearing level but within the irritation zone of dogs. Like a dog whistle that is silent to humans, dogs respond to the high-frequency sound-wave vibrations coming from the wheels.

Another theory is that the rotation of pedaling feet means kicking heels to a dog. Flailing feet is a form of attack on the dog's security. Still another theory is that a bicycle intrudes upon a dog's territory and, unlike the massive bulk of an automobile, its slow-moving, lightweight body can be attacked. Besides that, the biker himself is in a vulnerable position astride his flimsy machine and can be harassed easily. One more theory is that the simple movement of a bicycle on the road is a challenge to a dog to run it down, to compete with the rolling wheels, and to scare it into a vanquished wreck.

Whatever the case, the dogs outnumber the theories. Some dogs stare and yawn at a passing biker. Others stare and wait to attack until the biker has passed midpoint. Still others leap to a frontal charge at the first sound of rolling wheels. No two dogs are alike. Only unpredictability is shared among the canines.

Dogs in the city are as bothersome as elsewhere. However, dogs in the country are the ones that are usually unchained and allowed to roam free. They are the ones who see fewer strangers, let alone bicyclists, during the day and are apt to run after foreigners on first scent and sight. Dogs in the country are the enemy.

The theories on how best to handle dogs that attack bikers are as numerous as the theories of why dogs attack. Borrowing a method from mailmen, some bikers carry a can of Halt in their handlebar bags. When a dog growls, barks, and tries to run down the bike, the rider takes the aerosol can and sprays the dog in the face. Normally, this pepper-gas type of defense stops a dog at once.

However, the drawbacks to anti-dog sprays are several. Mailmen and bikers who use it find that a sprayed dog may occasionally become enraged and continue the atttack, or his hostility, growing as a consequence of the first spraying, may become more and more uncontrollable each time they pass. In other words, if you plan to ride repeatedly past a particularly troublesome dog, spraying the dog each time may worsen rather than improve the situation. On the other hand, if you plan a route for one-time riding, an anti-dog spray may be handy.

Another disadvantage to the sprays is that by the time you reach into the front bag, retrieve the can, aim, and fire the spray accurately, the dog has either already done his damage or is intimidating you so much you can't control the bike much less the spray can.

Kicking at a dog with your heels only induces more anger and challenge in the dog's attack. Avoid kicking. Besides, it takes your feet off the pedals and reduces control over your riding. Also, avoid turning your front wheel into the dog. This serves only to anger the dog more and, like kicking, steals control from your bike. If dog and front wheel meet, you take a spill for certain.

Some bikers immediately stop riding and get off their bikes when they approach a barking dog. By walking the bike into and out of a dog's territory, whether it's a farmhouse or corner tree, the chances of a dog's attacking are greatly reduced. This method has worked well for me, though one dog in particular continues to harass me even when I'm on the ground. This method takes time, encompasses a wide span of territory before and after the dog's perch, and in effect shamelessly admits that the dog wins.

If you have more pride than this allows for, the two most effective methods of dog control that I've found take less time and effort. The first is simply outright violence and authoritarianism. If a dog comes running and barking at you, maintain your speed and course until you see that he means business. Then slow down, take your air pump, and bop the monster on the head. The hit doesn't have to be brutal or even hard, just enough to let the animal know who's in charge. Circle the dog and tap him again if necessary. You do run the risk that the dog may respond more aggressively, but that risk is slight. The far greater majority of the time the dog stops running and barking and waits until you move on. Being kind to animals runs second to defending yourself against chomp marks on your calves.

The other method I've found effective is startlingly simple. *Roar!* The day I discovered this was one of angry frustration at being harassed by dogs one too many times. A semilarge black mongrel ran at me from the porch steps of a house in the Kansas plains. I turned to his barking and saw him racing toward me. I maintained course and speed, but when he closed the gap toward ultimate confrontation I turned and bellowed the loudest African growling roar this side of the Nile River. To my utter amazement, the dog skidded to a stop, choked a bark, and turned in a circle. He wasn't going to tangle with this Tyrannosaurus rex. I rode on, slightly embarrassed but totally triumphant.

OTHER ANIMALS

Normally, bikers have no trouble with any animal other than the dog. Cats are quick to scurry away from a bicycle coming down the road, although I remember one time a cat ran across my path in an alley. It ran between my wheels so that I could do nothing but run over it with my back tire. I expected squishy horror, but the cat merely rolled over as the wheel rolled over it. Then it stood up, shook its head, and continued its run across the alley.

In the city, cats and dogs are virtually the only animals that are seen. In the country far more animals are there, but pose little problem for bikers. No animal, including the misunderstood wolf, attacks a man, let alone a biker, unless the animal is helplessly cornered or it is rabid. Occasionally, a biker meets a stray cow on the road (if you do, be sure to give the cow the complete right of way) or someone on horseback. If you approach a horseback rider from the rear, shout or ring a bell to warn the rider and the horse that you are approaching. Don't startle either one.

A squirrel or chipmunk might dash across the road from one nut hatch to another. If one does cross your path, don't panic and swerve the front wheel so much that you lose balance and fall. Maintain your composure and direction. The chances of your hitting the scurrying bushy tail are astronomically slim.

Cattle in a field often spot you coming. One by one each head lifts up and before long all eyes are on you. Sometimes they stand up and follow you. Don't worry. You'll outpace them. Besides, they can't go any farther than the wire fence that separates them from the road.

The large wild animals are seldom seen at close range. Even if they are, they pose no problem and will probably be the first to run away. Deer, moose, bears, antelopes, and the others stay away from noisy traffic. Porcupines, raccoons, woodchucks, and beavers can be spotted from the road, but they, too, offer no challenge. Never but never corner a skunk. Skunks are peaceful, harmless animals. However, their lone weapon of defense is devastating. If they find you aggressive and spray you, you're in deep smelly trouble for the next three or four days at the least.

Bikers who camp may spot a bobcat or bear rummaging through garbage and unpacked food. Bobcats scurry off faster than bears, but neither one will hurt you if you pose no threat to them. Best deterrent to bobcats and bears is to have no garbage. Repack your food in plastic bags, put them in your saddlebags or pillowcase, and hang the bags or case high on an isolated tree limb. Campers should also be careful not to put their salty hands on the wheels of their bikes. I've seen the remains of a tire chewed to pieces by a raccoon that was after the smell and taste of salt.

NIGHT RIDING

A bicycle is a daytime vehicle. Use it when the sun is up and park it when the sun goes down. Riding at night can be unnecessarily dangerous. Not only that, but you simply can't see. You can't see rocks and nails on the road or downy woodpeckers and circling crows on the landscape. Worse yet, people have a difficult time seeing you.

Some nights when the moon is full in a starry sky and the road is flat and unobstructed by trees, riding at night is both safe and enjoyable. However, on the whole, night riding is not recommended. First of all, bicycle lights are totally inadequate. Besides that, they add extra weight to your bike, especially the lights run by a generator that rubs against the rim of the front wheel.

The French-designed night light that attaches to your arm or leg is good within its own theoretical context, but in practice this light that shines white to the front and red to the rear is still inadequate by itself. The up-and-down motion of this light as you ride can be confusing to a motorist, though this confusion does serve to perk up a driver's interest.

Riding at night demands too much attention to preserving your safety. The result is that nearly all your concern is to remain out of accidents rather than to enjoy the ride. Whether you're riding in the city or country, plan to avoid the night hours on the road.

However, if from some sense of adventure or dire necessity you must ride at night, do so with sufficient warning to others on the road and for your own self-protection. Sufficient warning means to gear yourself up with ample lighting and reflection. Do not rely on only one source of safety. Put yourself in the place of a motorist. Even with his powerful headlights, to him a biker is merely a slice of the darkness, another distortion in the night that could just as well be an isolated freak reflection up ahead. The driver may even have night blindness. At automobile speeds a motorist runs the roads with the presumption that only cars and trucks use the same road. His scope of vision shrinks to a fraction of what he can see in the daylight.

This means that your bike must be extremely well lighted. For night riding combine all the gadgets and safety tricks you can use. Put long strips of reflection tape on your fenders if you have them, on your handlebars, and on both front and rear forks. Stick strips of this Scotchlite to the back of your jacket or shirt. This reflective tape can be seen by motorists 600 feet away. The white tape, not the yellow or red, is best.

Make certain you have at least a three-inch red reflector for your bike. Attach the most powerful front light you can find to your handlebars. Wear an arm or leg flashlight. Wear the whitest clothing you have.

A biker is a daytime animal. When he ventures into the night, he ventures into high risk.

WIND

All bikers are subject to Aeolus, the King of the Winds. If Aeolus favors the biker, all is well. If Aeolus fights the biker, all is a struggle.

Nearly 90 per cent of your energy is burned up plowing through the wind. The other 10 per cent or so, studies show, is used to balance out the wheel friction on the road from the weight of the bike. The wind is a critical factor in any bike hike. In the country, wind can push a biker along a highway up to a twenty or more miles an hour increase in speed. On the other hand, a headwind can drain a biker's strength and reduce his mileage drastically.

Drop handlebars are designed not only to squeeze the most power from your body but also to reduce the wind resistance your body would produce otherwise in an upright position. Always crouch into the lowest position in order to fight a strong headwind. The more wind you prevent hitting your body, the easier is your ride.

A route along banks of trees on either side of the road is worth following on a windy day. The trees deflect much of the wind that sweeps over the land. However, routes that follow the open plains or long stretches of farm fields on windy days are the ones to consider carefully. If the wind follows your line of direction, you have a friend in the sky. If a strong wind bucks you all the way, it is often better to wait another day, especially for the morning hours when the winds are generally softer.

Circumstances may dictate that you must ride against a strong wind in the country or mountains. To avoid constant frustration and fatigue, set your mind into a lower gear. Remind yourself that you cannot possibly gain as much distance and speed fighting the wind as on calmer days. Then resign yourself to the fact. You cannot fight a strong headwind with curses and incantations. You merely defeat yourself entirely and ruin the day even further.

Too many bikers fight the wind in their heads. Inevitably, they lose. They constantly complain the hours away, throw their bikes to the ground in anger, and grow unnecessarily exhausted both psychologically and physically. Keep a cool head. Remain in the lower gears and let the bike do the work. Keep plodding along. Expect short gains, not gigantic leaps forward.

On windy days in the mountains where the roads take you close to cliffs, be extracautious. A gusty wind can rush down a mountainside and tumble you off the road. Stay away from the cliff side of the highway. Often sudden updrafts can bend up and over a road with surprising force.

Group riders have the advantage over loners when facing a strong headwind. If you're in a group on the open plains, trade off every fifteen minutes for the lead position. The lead rider wedges the wind away from the others. To be effective the group must remain quite bunched together so that the wind is deflected without having time to seep back full force in front of every other rider. Depending on the terrain and the traffic, riding against the wind in groups can be done effectively in single file or in a tight pie-shape wedge. The bikers must be confident of each other though to provide everyone with the first necessity—safety.

Some bikers make wings, with lightweight tubing for the frame and nylon for the sheet. The wings are tied to the back and waist and are used to increase the pushing power of a back wind. As the exotica of biking enlarges, so will the number of winged bikers appearing on the windy roads.

RAIN

Sooner or later every bike hiker faces a cloudful of rain. It happens to the best of us and there's nothing a biker can do to avoid the drizzle blues. Some bikers plod on through the showers no matter what, while others stop pedaling at the first sign of shadow.

Generally, it's better not to ride in the rain. The streets and highways become slippery and muddy. Cars and trucks increase the danger of wet roads. The darker skies make visibility more difficult. Unless a road has an exceptionally wide shoulder to ride on, you get sprayed from the wheels of passing traffic. You also find that in the end the effort you expend avoiding the puddles and splashes is nowhere near the reward of a day of good biking.

You can wear a plastic raincoat or a poncho while you ride in the rain. If you do, be sure that either one is bulky enough so that it fits over the bike but not so loose and flappy that it can catch in the spokes and chain, a disaster for both you and your two-wheeler. Remember that if you do want to wear a raincoat you must carry it along with you all the hours it is not raining. That means extra weight.

Summer rain is not cold. Bikers can ride through the showers with only their standard clothes for the road. If you are caught in the rain, keep your hat pulled down over your forehead and sunglasses. The sunglasses keep the raindrops from blobbing your eyesight.

Fenders or mudguards can eliminate the continuous ring of water whirling up from both the front and back wheel. Fenders keep your clothes clean, too. However, most bikers find that the extra weight of fenders is not worth the results.

Often the best way to face a rain is under a tree or in a gas station. Simply pull into some shelter at the first sign of drizzle and wait it out. This is the time to snack on peaches and gorp and watch the cars that could be splashing you wet speed by. When the rain stops, it's a good idea to wait another fifteen or twenty minutes to allow the water to run off the road and evaporate as much as possible. Even though the rain is not falling, cars and trucks continue to splatter water from their wheels awhile.

Experienced bike hikers have found that fighting the wet weather is ultimately a waste of time. They either hole up in a town for the rest of the day, if the rain shows no sign of letup, or, if it's only a drizzle, they wait it out under a tree. Such bikers can easily make up the lost time on dry ground and at the same time eliminate soaked clothing and the risk of accidents.

If you do get drenched by a cloudburst, be sure to relubricate your bike at the earliest possible dry moment. This is important. Do it while you have it in mind. Water washes oil from the moving parts that need it.

First, wipe the bike dry of water. Clean off the mud and dirt. Then lubricate all the vital moving parts as suggested in the manual for your bike. After a rain, lubricating the bearings in the gear sprocket, the hubs, the chain, and the derailleurs is especially important.

MOUNTAIN CLIMBING

The most terrifying thought about mountain riding is the word "mountain." Think "hill." The Green Mountains of Vermont, the White Mountains of New Hampshire, the Appalachias, the Rockies, the Sierra Nevadas, the Pacific Coast Range, and the others are merely super hillocks.

A slow, steady cadence gets you and any other bike hiker up and over any mountain. It may take a day or two or three, but it's possible. Presumably, you are in good physical shape before you challenge a super hillock and, accordingly, you have planned the contents of your saddlebags for the lightest possible weight.

The first two tricks to mountain climbing on a bicycle are to set yourself psychologically for the effort and to let the gears on the bike do the work. Pedaling up a mountainside is work indeed. It takes much difficult, strenuous exertion and it takes time. Acknowledge to yourself both the grind and the time it does take. Set your psychological goal as high as the mountaintop, but set your psychological pace on a moderate, realistic time schedule. Project how long the climb may take to reach the top and then plod along up the hill. Expect great achievements of yourself, but not the impossible. It is impossible to speed up a mountain, but it is not impossible to inch your way to the top. Remove the cumulative frustration of not reaching the top faster by not expecting yourself to reach the summit fast in the first place. Climb the mountain with one circle of the pedals at a time.

Keep your eyes away from the mountaintop. Its distance or steepness may be defeating every time you look at it. Keep your head down. Look at the road in front of you. In time, any biker can flatten any mountain.

Next, let the bike be your conquering vehicle. Use the lowest gears necessary. The hero is the one who makes the top, not the exhausted, defeated soul who strained in too high a gear. Generally, a rhythm between full steam ahead and a turtle crawl is the best. Applying full energy at the outset only expends prematurely a biker's potential. Poking along only drains enthusiasm and leads to self-defeat. A moderate rhythm is the secret.

Keep your eyes on the road just ahead and pedal at your own speed. If you're in a group, it's better to pull ahead or drop behind by riding to fit your energy and cadence. This is not the time to worry about togetherness. If you strain to keep up with the others or ease up to stay with those who have different paces, you drain yourself either way.

An explosion of power at the base of a mountain climb is wasteful. At the same time, too easy a pace at the outset can discourage a biker halfway up the mountain.

Some super hillocks like the Green Mountains in Vermont are wavy, with many up-and-down sections through small valleys. Others like the Rockies in Colorado or the Sierra Nevadas in California can have upgrades that last ten, twenty and more miles. Tioga Pass, between Lee Vining and Yosemite National Park, is 9,946 feet high in the Sierra Nevadas. Bikers have climbed up and over the pass.

Conquering mountains requires stamina that is well planned to last the entire climb. If necessary, take rests frequently. Stop by the side of the road and lean standing up against a tree or sit or lie down with your legs stretched outward. Avoid the possibility of cramps. Don't sit with your knees bent.

Mountain climbing demands extra energy of your body. Maintain the supply of energy by eating at regular intervals whatever high-energy food you have. Don't wait until you're hungry. By then it's too late. The same is true of water. Your body demands great quantities of water to cool the heat that is generated when your muscles work strenuously. Drink small quantities, but drink frequently at regular intervals.

At times you may face an especially steep upgrade when you are particularly tired. Don't be so proud that you refuse to get off your bike and walk it awhile, if not to the very top. Think in terms of the over-all climb. Regulate the outflow of your energy. Walking the bike when the lowest gear is not low enough is sensible.

Bear in mind that sharp mountain curves can be dangerous. On narrow, curving horseshoe roads be aware that a motorist may come speeding around a blind curve behind you. The curve may block the noise of the car from you. If you can neither see nor hear a car coming behind you and you're too far left into the lane of traffic, the situation is set for an accident.

On sharp curves stay as close to the mountainside as possible. Depending on the situation, sometimes it is safer to cross to the other side of the road and ride against the traffic. If the traffic is nowhere in sight on long straight stretches (and each of those last words is equally important), ride in the center of the highway. The center of the road has fewer rocks, keeps you away from the updrafts of cliffs, and provides you with a less claustrophobic feeling.

Mountain roads that are cut roughly through the terrain and are left free of vegetation produce small rock slides now and then. Other than with quick wits, bikers cannot prevent a slide from hitting their machines, nor are they protected as in a car. Still, the rocks, pebbles, and sand are ever-present obstacles on mountain climbs. Constantly be alert to debris on the road. The one and a quarter-inch tires on a 10-speed bicycle offer little resistance to puncturing pebbles.

MOUNTAIN COASTING

Rejoice that super hillocks have downhill sides. What goes up must come down. Normally, bikers stop at the summit of a mountain to rest. Do so even if you feel exhilarated and are ready to plunge to the valley floor. After a long, hard climb you need time to rejuvenate your body and spirit no matter how strong the vibrations that tingle through your arms and legs. Give yourself the benefit of a five- to ten-minute rest before you start a long downhill race. It could easily prevent an accident.

Obviously, mountain coasting is a mink-soft luxury compared to mountain climbing. Still, coasting down a steep incline has its risks. Take the few extra minutes and precaution to prevent any mishaps.

A rest at the mountaintop should help you put into perspective what lies ahead. While you're resting, check your bike for any unusual noises or malfunctioning parts noticeable on the way up. Repair them before you apply any speed to the bike, as you do downhill.

Check both your front and rear brakes to see that they work perfectly. Repeat: perfectly. Remove from the rims any water or oil that may have splattered on. More than likely you didn't need your brakes on the way up. On the way down they are absolutely essential.

Tighten your saddlebag straps if they are loose or your cargo may vibrate you off balance at high speed. Check your tires for any sludge or pebbles imbedded between the treads and remove any foreign material that may cause damage.

On the downgrade lean low into the wind. Keep your hands on the brakes at all times. Shift into the highest gear you have. Keep your sunglasses on so the wind doesn't smear your vision with the moisture in your eyes or sting away your vision with sand. Suppress the temptation to speed as fast as you can. By pedaling most of the time you coast, you can tell in general how fast you're traveling. If you have no pressure against the chain as you pedal in tenth gear, you're going much too fast. If you have an odometer, you can tell by the speed of the clicking whether you're moving faster than ever before.

Bikers on the downgrade can race out of control unless they take these few precautions. On a long downhill course your speed accumulates almost without your knowing it. It's extremely deceiving. Bikers can quickly accelerate to sixty and seventy miles per hour and still feel as if they were traveling a mere thirty or forty.

The thrill of flying down a mountainside after such an arduous climb is something you earned and deserve, but unless you keep the thrill under control you're playing with an explosive situation. A single rock that comes at you too fast for you to maneuver around may tumble you into oblivion.

Apply the brakes in spurts as you coast. This sustains you at a uniform speed. Otherwise, enjoy the excitement to the fullest. A downhill ride is one of the supreme pleasures of bike hiking. You slice through the wind you're creating yourself. You fly over the earth in one of the easiest intoxications you've ever had, a reward for the upgrade you climbed and a reminder that this seductive, light-footed, zooming fun is what it's all about. Long live the back side of mountains!

7

DESERT RIDING

Of all the landscapes bikers plan to ride through, the desert is perhaps the most terrifying and the least appreciated. The image of the desert as a reject of Mother Earth doesn't help, nor do the cartoons of dehydrated prospectors crawling across the endless sands for a sip of water and the sanity of civilization.

The image and reality of the desert are less terrifying if that exotic netherland in the western third of our nation is understood a little in advance of confronting it. The confrontation between desert and biker is real indeed if the biker looks upon this countryside as dead real estate to be tolerated on his own terms. Surprise. The desert, as no other type of territory, without exception deals with you on its terms.

Don't be frightened off. The desert certainly need not defeat your plans to venture into its realm or even to cross it entirely on two wheels. Rest assured that desert riding can be safe as well as enjoyable. Still, it's a wise pedaler who knows his place.

RESPECT THE DESERT

From a distance the desert may appear to uninitiated bikers as seductively easy terrain to ride. The roads look fairly flat and straight, the horizon unobstructed, the skies clear and calm. Somehow the mystery of the desert seems to be less its warnings than its indecipherable appeal. It seems to be a forthright type of place. Dangers are less evident than the cliffs in mountain areas or the storms in the Midwest. Those placid scenes in *Arizona Highways* don't evoke any sirens of calamity. All the world seems at peace with itself in the desert.

Be careful of such one-dimensional evaluations. To Westerners, familiarity with the desert brings with it a caution if not a liking. To Easterners used to mountains only four or five thousand feet high and states merely two or three hundred miles wide, rumors of the desert never loom as large as the reality.

The desert must be approached with respect. It is large, subtle, and in command. The desert can be ruthless in ambushing unsuspecting bikers with heat and thirst, let alone a sense of defeat and fright as hundred-mile valleys envelop two-wheelers like two grains of sand. Because of this, bikers must plan ahead carefully and ride with caution.

By all means, ride the desert, but do so with humility and restraint. Keep your goals in tune with the territory. You are entering a domain in which you are completely exposed to the elements, in which fifty miles, and sometimes more, may stretch between settlements. Pay attention to the advice of the local people. Verify your maps with everyone you meet on the way. Ride with enthusiasm, but whatever you do temper it with a healthy respect for a country that can devour you with impunity on one of its glass-flat highways.

WHAT IS THE DESERT?

Desert is land that receives less than ten inches of rain each year. Probably the best-known desert is the Sahara, the largest desert in the world. The Sahara extends across the top of Africa for 3,200 miles, varying north and south from 800 to 1,400 miles, and is a big reason why one fifth of the land surface of the world is desert.

Within its own borders, desert is far from homogeneous. It includes high plateaus as well as below-sea-level valleys, mountainsides of yucca cacti as well as lowlands of sand dunes. In some areas sagebrush extends to the horizons. In others, rich stains of green copper and red iron color the earth for miles. The variety of animal and plant life is staggering, ranging from scorpions to mule deer and wild lupine to century-year-old saguaros.

The desert is hard, raw earth country. The great monoliths of Monument Valley in Utah and the lava flows west of Needles, California, are examples of the rugged simplicity. Sand dunes do exist, but they are a fraction of the real desert. Some are located near El Centro and Death Valley in California. Sand dunes near Winnemucca, Nevada, rise to seventy-five feet and spread forty miles long and ten miles wide. However, the snow-colored dunes of White Sands National Monument near Alamogordo, New Mexico, belie categorizing the desert too easily. White Sands National Monument is not made of sand but of granulated gypsum.

Don't presume anything about the desert. Once I was among a half-dozen people who watched an exuberant member of the Adventurers Club walk across the floor of Death Valley in August when the temperature was 128 degrees in the shade of a palm tree at Furnace Creek and the humidity was 24 per cent, unusually high. The man walked only six miles and collapsed the third and final time from heat exhaustion. Don't plan to ride your bike in Death Valley in August.

WHERE IS THE DESERT?

In the United States, the desert by and large is located between the Rocky Mountains and the Sierra Nevada Range, even though other areas such as the Oklahoma Panhandle and eastern New Mexico look like classic desert. The Great American Desert is divided into several sections, including the Great Basin Desert, the Mohave Desert, the Painted Desert, and the Sonoran Desert.

The Great Basin touches Nevada, Utah, Colorado, Oregon, Idaho, and Wyoming. The Mohave is located in California and Nevada, the Painted Desert lies in eastern Arizona, Colorado, Utah, and New Mexico, the Sonoran in Arizona.

Desert country stretches nearly the entire distance from

the Mexican to the Canadian borders, from California to Washington. The West encompasses vast territory. Each of the deserts includes a variety of countrysides and altitudes. The Mohave, for example, has Death Valley at 282 feet below sea level, but it also has 3,000-foot plateaus in other parts of California. Paying attention to the altitude is important in selecting desert routes. Also important is the length of summer. Summer in the Great Basin Desert lasts two to three months. In the Mohave summer lasts six months, in the Sonoran Desert seven to nine months.

Two-wheel riders on long-term trips eventually must cross some desert country if they want to cross the West. Knowing a few basics about desert travel can prevent unnecessary fears and minimize the remote chance of problems.

THAT HOT SOLAR EYE

The sun is no biker's friend on a cloudless summer day in the desert. Temperatures rise into the 100s. Asphalt that is poorly laid can soften and create squishy riding conditions. Exposed skin can be burned to blisters. Dehydration can creep upon the best-trained rider and demolish him. The only safeguard is sound prevention. Cures are too late for an enjoyable trip.

Fortunately, the heat in the desert is not as devastating as the 100-degree temperatures may appear in print, though it certainly is a factor to respect. The relatively low humidity offsets the intense discomfort that results from the combination of high temperatures and high humidity found in the Midwest and South.

Mountain ranges that border the desert act as barriers to moisture-laden clouds. As a result, towns such as Barstow, California, receive about four inches of rain a year and have air dry and bearable on rainless days. Nevertheless, temperatures in the 100s are nothing to sneeze at. It's unlikely that you'll ride into the 134 degrees that was recorded at Greenland Ranch, Death Valley, on July 10, 1913, the most reliable "hottest" reading in the world. Still, temperatures anywhere above 100 degrees in the open desert are furnace enough.

Hot desert riding is certainly possible if your pace is slow and steady. Desert wind or the wind you create by riding does cool your body. Besides that, the motion of your body as you pedal fights the sluggishness that can overcome any deadbeat inactivity resulting from heat. This riding effort though must be reduced considerably.

One time in the Arizona desert I was covering about twenty miles an hour for the first half of the morning. At 9:00 A.M. the thermometer in a lonely gas-station coffee shop read 84 degrees. By noon, when the temperature had risen to 104 degrees, I dropped my pace to about ten miles per hour as a precaution, even though I wanted to press harder. It was a decision that paid off in the long run.

WHAT TO WEAR

The constant downpour of sun rays in the desert demands that you wear clothes that protect you. Some clothes are optional, others absolutely necessary. The one item that is necessary in the desert is a hat.

One of the best models is a white cotton tennis hat. As mentioned earlier, this hat is designed with a long full-circle bill that shields your forehead, eyes, and part of your cheeks and neck. The underside of the bill is green to reduce the reflection of sunlight from the road and surrounding countryside. The cotton material "breathes" and is soft. Being white, it reflects nearly 90 per cent of the sunlight, thus decreasing the heat intake. Another advantage is that you can soak the hat in water at a gas station, flop it wet on your head, and cycle down the road with a cool head.

A similar trick is to take a small bath towel, soak it in water, place it lengthwise over your head and neck and shoulders, and secure it on your head with your hat. As you ride, the wind blows through the towel cooling your body, and you have the covering to protect you from the sun. The style is as ancient as the Arabs.

White is the best color for desert riding. Avoid the dark colors since they tend to absorb the light's heat. Extremely thin materials are not satisfactory either. They allow the sun rays to penetrate and do not retain the moisture of your body as well as do thicker materials like medium-weight cotton or wool. Remember that the desert-wise Arabs for centuries used the wool of their sheep for their clothes.

A good pair of sunglasses that wrap closely to your forehead and cheekbones are needed to protect your eyes from constant glare. They prevent you from squinting and developing headaches.

Wear your long-sleeved shirt or blouse at all times. (Girls without blouses create accidents.) A bare back under the desert sun is an invitation to disaster. No matter how tempting or logical it seems to remove your shirt, don't. The sun can boil your back. The dry air sponges away your perspiration. Your energy drains away as if a plug had been removed.

I remember a report of two men who landed an airplane in an emergency in the desert. Against the advice of his friend, one man removed his shirt because he figured the best way to get cool was to shed his clothes. Then in mid-afternoon he walked across the desert floor to get help. The other man remained under the shade of the downed plane. The man who challenged the desert was found dead, his face and back scorched like burned paint. The man who kept his senses and his shirt survived.

Lesson: when riding your bike in the desert keep your shirt on. It doesn't make sense on the surface but, like drinking hot tea instead of iced tea in hot country, it works better.

Your legs may need to be protected if you have fair skin and have had little exposure to the sun. If you do substitute long pants for cut-offs or shorts, wear light-colored slacks that are loose so they won't constrict your pedaling. However, your legs may not need as much covering as other parts of your body. Long pants can be considered optional if your riding hours are reasonable.

WHEN TO RIDE

The best riding time in the desert is early morning. On a typical day the sun shines in a clear sky. The air is crisp and invigorating. The wind is not yet astir. The horizons are full of colors and the land is a stretch of promise. The combination is difficult to top.

Get up at the break of dawn and definitely be on the road before sunrise. Not only are you refreshed then and at the peak of your pedaling powers, but the desert is at its most inviting. Normally, the stiffling heat of the previous day has cooled during the night. In the desert it is common for the temperature to drop thirty degrees or more once the sun has fallen. The 105-degree heat during the afternoon may shrink to 70 degrees overnight. The following morning, you'll wake up to an ideal riding temperature.

Gradually, you have to reduce your effort as the hour moves toward noon. Most often the hottest temperature of the day is recorded between 12:30 and 2:30 P.M. To avoid these hours on the road, plan your stopover points a day or two in advance and stick to them. That way you can ride into a town near noon, find a cool shady spot inside or out, and wait out the scorching hours. Depending on your stamina and general plans, you may wish to ride only the morning hours anyway.

If you plan to ride later in the afternoon, heat is only one problem to be aware of. Wind is the natural by-product of heat. As the sun progresses across the sky, it heats the earth and air. Hot air rises, cooler air rushes below. The net effect is an increase in the movement of air. Wind. Be prepared for desert wind, especially in the afternoon.

More often than not, the wind dies down after the sun drops toward the west and finally disappears behind the mountains. Riding in the late afternoon and twilight can be extremely pleasant in the desert. However, be sure that your destination is nearby and well within the time limit before darkness.

Bicycling at night in the desert, or anywhere, for that matter, is not recommended unless necessary. Lights for bikes are extremely inefficient and can be bewildering to car drivers unfamiliar with bikers. Also, avoiding glass and nails on the road is more difficult at night. Repairing a flat tire, or dealing with any other bike problem, in the dark is a double effort in frustration. Eliminate that contingency by riding in the daylight.

WINDS AND STORMS

The afternoon winds that blow when the desert floor heats up follow general patterns. Bikers can plan for the wind by asking the local people about the usual direction of the wind and the speed with which it washes through the valleys and towns. Sometimes a call to the local airport or weather service can give you even more precise information, as well as forecasts for the next day or two.

Generally, the prevailing wind direction in the desert is from west to east, as it is across the entire nation. Mountain ranges that, for example, angle a desert valley southwest–northeast funnel the wind from the southwest. Topological maps can give you hints of general wind directions by indicating the lay of the land.

If you're riding east, the west wind is an ally and helps push you along the road. On the other hand, if you're riding west, the wind coming directly at you demands more energy output on your part and slows your speed considerably.

Remember that on the desert floor no rows of eucalyptus trees buffer the wind as it sweeps unimpeded through a valley. No buildings or buttes or mounds of boulders stand between you and that unseen foe that never seems to relent when you want it to. Traveling west, it's you against the wind. Your over-all plan then should be to ride early in the morning and wait out the west wind in the afternoon. Plan ahead for the wind just as you would plan ahead where and when to fill up a gas tank if you were driving a car through the Painted Desert.

However, always be prepared for the unexpected. The wind is as untamed as it is unseen. One time riding west in the Arizona desert I covered ninety miles from 6:30 A.M. until noon. By the time I was on the far side of Kingman, the wind had been blowing at about twelve to fifteen miles per hour directly into my front wheel. I struggled on to Yucca, an old oasis of about one hundred souls that Interstate 40 has divided in half. My destination for the day, Needles, California, was another forty miles, but the wind had increased to about eighteen to twenty miles per hour head-on.

Exhausted, I stopped in Yucca for the day and night. That evening a violent thunderstorm roared through the huge valley. Rain fell in a series of short heavy cloudbursts. Lightning flashed open the sky and thunder cracked the night. The display equaled first-class storms of the Midwest. All night the wind blew against my rattling motel window.

Normally, the night calms the wind, but the following morning I heard it blowing hard against the desert floor. Immediately, my spirits dropped at the prospect of facing that energy-sapping onslaught again. I thought I'd have to spend the day in Yucca (not known for its fascination and zest) and wait out this wild Maria that was blowing more gray storm clouds and depression my way.

After weighing the alternatives, I decided that plowing through the hostile winds at forty miles a day to the next spot of civilization was better than Yucca, Arizona. I packed, saddled my trusty mount, yanked my hat down snug and tight, and pedaled onto the highway. To my utter amazement, the wind had switched directions during the night. Now it blew from the east—at my back.

My spirits rebounded at once. With the wind behind me I zinged down the forty miles to Needles in an hour and a half, racing the new crop of dark clouds gathering behind me and for ten miles keeping pace with a Santa Fe freight train that paralleled the old U.S. Route 66.

Lesson: the desert is full of surprises, not all of them bad.

HEAT EXHAUSTION AND HEAT STROKE

The subtle dangers of the desert in summer must not be ignored. A combination of oppressive heat and overexertion can topple you from your bike almost as fast as an oversize curb. The continuous downbeat of the sun as you pedal across a 105-degree desert floor can be devastating if you pedal too fast. Be aware of the symptoms of the two forms of heat attack that can creep upon you or anyone else if precautions are not taken.

Heat exhaustion or prostration, although very serious, is less dangerous than heat stroke. If you are riding in the desert or merely standing in the sun for prolonged periods and suddenly feel dizzy, weak, nauseated, you may be suffering from heat exhaustion. In severe cases that are not caught early, you may even lose consciousness. Your pulse beat increases rapidly up to 200 heartbeats a minute. Your skin turns pale and you perspire heavily.

If someone in your group shows these symptoms, or if you're alone, stop riding immediately. Find shade under desert cactus, sagebrush, storm-drain pipes, behind bluffs, anywhere. Whatever you do, get out of the sun. Find the coolest spot possible. Then drink (don't gulp) as much water as you think replenishes your body. Swallow salt tablets to replace whatever salt your body has lost through perspiration. Lie down and raise your feet in order to force the blood toward your head.

Heat exhaustion can ambush you. Prevent the attack by riding slowly, drinking lots of water, and resting frequently.

Heat stroke is far more dangerous. In this attack you stop perspiring completely, which, in turn, raises your body temperature to as high as 110 degrees. Your cooling system has broken down completely. At the same time your heartbeat rises dramatically, your skin turns red and dry, you feel exceptionally hot, and you may lapse into unconsciousness or a coma.

A heat stroke demands faster action than heat exhaustion. The victim absolutely must be taken to the coolest possible place to reduce body temperature and, if possible, put in cold water. If he is conscious, the salt content of his body must be replenished. Speed is of the utmost importance.

Bikers need not be overly anxious about heat exhaustion and heat stroke if they use good sense and do not attempt too much. However, if they presume upon the apparent innocence and simplicity of the desert without respecting its harshness, they may fall victim.

SANDSTORMS

Sandstorms can sweep across a highway and quickly incapacitate both biker and bike. If you see a storm coming or hear of one from the local people or radio, stop and cover your bike with newspaper, plastic raincoat, plastic bags, tarps, anything to shield the gears, derailleurs, and movable parts that are lubricated. If you are caught in a sandstorm, thoroughly clean all movable parts of your bike and relubricate. It is essential to remove all the sand before you continue to ride.

Often when the more severe sandstorms are imminent, the state highway patrol broadcasts warnings and sets up temporary roadblocks until the storm has passed. A sandstorm can pit windshields and the paint of a car, but it can literally grind a bicycle to a stop.

Sandstorms and duststorms begin with winds that slip across the desert floor at fifteen miles per hour. A mild storm has twenty-mile-per-hour winds, a severe storm, thirty-mile-per-hour winds. All desert winds don't constitute a sandstorm or duststorm, though when the winds do register high on a wind gauge, sand and dust are blown up from the ground. Sandstorms normally raise sand particles only about two or three feet off the ground. (Ostrichs are said to have developed long necks to see over the sandstorms.) The sand is too heavy to fly much higher. Duststorms, however, can fill a sky.

Bikers in the desert often see whirlwinds and dust devils in the distance. These are harmless phenomena and usually dissipate in short time. They result from an irregular upward rush of heated air on calm days. Other than these dust devils, bikers don't have to worry much about the storms. Simply be aware of their possibility. Pay attention to any highway patrol warnings that you see or hear and abide by them.

FLASHFLOODS

Flashfloods fall into the same category as sandstorms. They exist in the desert, but a biker's chances of meeting one are

extremely rare and they should not alone be reason to fea
riding across the desert.

The warning for a flashflood sometimes follows the pre
diction of extremely heavy rainfall in the desert mountain:
If a thundercloud breaks and rain fills the mountain canyon
and lowlands, flashfloods across the desert floor are possible

If you happen to be riding close to mountains or hills unde
dark clouds, pay attention to the possibility of flashflood.
Your warning on the open road is a deep thundering roar i
the distance. The intensity of the sound rises quickly. Th
earth may rumble like an earthquake. This sound is the ur
stoppable rush of walls of water thrashing down the ravine
and gorges. The water by this time has accumulated from a
the smaller mountain crevices that have meshed into large
canyons.

At the sound of such a warning, take every precaution t
move to high ground. Do not hide in a gulley or ravine. Wate
takes the line of least resistance. Take your bike and yourse
off the road and onto a bluff, the highest, closest one in sigh
Hurry.

A flashflood is one of the surprise disasters of nature. Wate
rushes in a torrent, completely untamed, down a canyon. I
a few seconds desert ground that was previously as dry a
a burro's bone is three feet under angry brown water. Th
flood lasts ten or fifteen minutes or more. Then about twent
minutes later, or less, the waters seep mysteriously into th
earth as if nothing had ever happened. The day continues a
before, except for the plant and animal life trapped in th
way.

Bikers should not worry too much about flashfloods, thoug
be alert for these warning signs: rainclouds over nearb
mountains or hills, ravines close to the road, the distant roa
of water, the tremors of the earth. If all these signs strin
together when you're riding the highway, climb to the highe
point at once.

WATER, COOL CLEAR WATER

About 72 per cent of the human body is water. The dr
desert air quickly evaporates much of this moisture fro

your body. Therefore, water must be replaced continually, especially when the physical exertion of riding a bicycle requires so much.

You can conserve the moisture in your body by wearing medium-weight shirts and a windbreaker. As previously warned, do not remove most of your clothes in the mistaken belief that this cools you off. It cools you off at first, but in the long run you lose moisture far faster to wind, dry air, and the sheer lack of clothing protection. Clothing helps retard the evaporation. Slow and steady pedaling, in contrast to fast and furious riding, helps prevent undue loss of moisture through perspiration. In addition, always rest in the shade under a bridge, beside a cactus, in a storm drain, behind a boulder, anywhere out of the sun.

When riding in the desert always carry at least two standard-size water jugs that fit onto the seat and down tubes of your bike. Fill them up at every opportunity, even if they are half full already. Never presume that a half-filled jug is sufficient until the next stop. Once I spotted a gas-station oasis in the distance. Even though I was thirsty, I decided not to drink all my water. It was good I didn't. The station was abandoned. I learned not to presume a water supply until I had it in hand.

Some bikers when they enter the desert carry an extra supply of water besides the two jugs. One trick is to use an empty plastic gallon or half-gallon milk container. Simply fill it with water and strap it to your bike rack. This provides an extra measure of security against parched lips, dehydration, and loss of energy.

However, keep in mind that water weighs a great deal. One gallon of water weighs 8.345 pounds. A half gallon of water weighs a little over four pounds. This additional weight makes a difference in your energy output, particularly up the long steep climbs.

I've found that two water jugs designed for bicycles are adequate in riding the summer desert. It's not an overabundance, or perhaps even plenty, but it is adequate if you ration yourself a certain number of swallows at each rest point.

To complement your water supply, carry along fruit that

is heavy with moisture. I use Thompson seedless grapes. Many times I'd take my allotted number of swallows of water, five or six, and then eat handfuls of grapes that I carry in my handlebar bag. Grapes are composed of 82 per cent water in addition to a high concentration of natural sugar for energy. Thompson seedless grapes end up as California raisins that many athletes eat for quick last-minute power. This combination of rationed water and grapes works well in the desert.

THOSE DECEIVING DISTANCES

The desert transforms fifteen miles into what appears to be five miles. The vast expanses of shallow valleys that stretch ahead play tricks on your perspective. Normally, you're used to tighter landscapes, with hills and trees that mark the distance. In the desert these marks rarely exist. What remains in the waterless oceans you ride through is a cluster of buildings that in the clean air and unobstructed surroundings appears a few miles ahead. Actually, the town is three or four times the distance you expect. Rely on your map for mileage between points.

I learned the hard way. Once in Arizona I rode into a valley and saw a town ahead. My spirits rose and so did my pedaling output. The town was obviously only about eight or nine miles away. I pedaled hard for the waiting shade, cold water, and something cool to eat. The miles passed but the town seemed as far away as before. Most of the ride was downhill so the town was in sight the entire time. It must have been closer to twenty-five miles away from the point from where I first saw it. By the time I reached it my spirits had shrunk to frustration and anger at the deception the desert played on me. My energy was drained.

If you ride into a similar situation, maintain your slow pace. Don't rush to a town that seems a short distance away. Calculate what you think the distance is to the town and then multiply it by three. Distances in the desert are difficult to overestimate.

KEEP OTHERS INFORMED

If you're riding alone, or even if you're in a small group, you may feel better if others know what your destination is and how long you expect to take to reach it. The major highways like Route 66 or Interstate 10 have enough traffic so that if you run into trouble someone is sure to drive by soon.

However, if your route takes you to some of the lesser traveled roads, you may wish to add an ounce of prevention by keeping others informed of your whereabouts.

A good method is to call the state highway patrol and let them know that you are biking from, say, Blythe, California, to Yuma, Arizona, that day. You expect to arrive there by four o'clock in the afternoon at the latest, and that if the office hasn't heard from you by about that time you may be in trouble along the route. Help can then be sent.

It's possible to set up a chain of protection this way all across the desert. However, be certain that you call the highway patrol upon your arrival at your stated destination. Without your follow-up call, the patrol may make you the center of a massive search.

THE SPECIAL BEAUTY

Take time to enjoy the exotic flavor of the desert. The stern beauty of such an arid land is in its browns and reds, the raw shapes of the mountains, and the strange life forms. As you ride look at the astounding horizons that encircle you. Enjoy the plants nearby, the royal desert lupine, golden gilia, sage, aster, yucca, cholla, hedgehog cactus, saguaro, creosote, piñon, junipers, octillo. Bike riding in the desert allows you to see that special beauty at close range. It's worth all the careful planning and effort the desert demands.

8

THE BIG ONE—ACROSS
THE COUNTRY

Second to around the world, the ultimate trip for the average biker is across the country. Coast to coast by bike and body is a thought for millions of bicyclists. It's a plan for thousands and an achievement for hundreds.

Don't abandon the idea of riding a two-wheeler from the Pacific to the Atlantic merely because only a select few have done it. The trip is within range of nearly anyone who has the time, the ambition, the bicycle, the stamina, good sense and good planning.

IT'S BEEN DONE

Even though you might think that the number of people who have bicycled across the country is equal to those who have walked on the moon, the trip is not that exotic. People have done it for the last seventy-five years. They do it now and they will in the future, especially since the current bicycle boom has yet to crest.

Eugene McPherson was the first person to cross the country on a bicycle in less than three weeks. He left Santa Monica, California, on September 1, 1949, and arrived in New York City 20 days, 4 hours, and 29 minutes later, though some serious bikers view this speedy time with suspicion.

A few bikers ride across the North American Continent

in about thirty days if all goes well and the weather is good. That's averaging about a hundred miles a day. Some bikers stop a week or so to visit friends in, say, Colorado or Arkansas and that adds more days to the over-all time. Others take two months or more, some even the entire summer to cruise the back roads and see the sights along the way.

It's impossible to estimate the number of bikers who travel across country. Some say about one hundred try it each year, but the figure is probably much higher now. Today, long-distance biking is a more widespread adventure, a summer happening for many young people and a refreshingly different vacation for the elders. Participants in the cross-country guided tours of the American Youth Hostels are increasing, as well as local groups that set off on the ultimate trip.

Biking on both coasts is far more advanced than in the South and Midwest. As a result, the percentage of bikers making the long trip to the opposite ocean increases.

(An even more exclusive trip is the one Dan and Lys Burden and June and Greg Siple are making. At last report, they had pedaled 5,000 miles of the 20,000-mile trip from Anchorage, Alaska, to Tierra del Fuego at the tip of South America. They figured $2,500 per person for the year-long bike hike. They also figured they are the only couples who have attempted such a trip.)

THE TIME IT TAKES

The most direct route from coast to coast takes a minimum of one full month for the average bike hiker. The distance from Boston to Los Angeles is 3,052 miles. At one hundred miles a day a bike trip takes thirty days. This schedule does not take into account the wind, rain, bike problems, side trips, accidents, detours, sightseeing, physical endurance, psychological staying power, and the will to finish.

A more realistic schedule for a cross-country trip is between six weeks and two months. This allows for days to rest, places to see, and time delays beyond your control. If you average between sixty-five and seventy-five miles a day, your pace can be sustained at a comparatively pleasant level without your feeling the necessity to trudge onward day after day. For shorter trips, averaging one hundred miles a day is within range of the average biker, but for a long-term trip that may cover weeks instead of merely days such a pace can be self-defeating for many.

An important consideration is to maintain a brisk pace. Racing across the country exhausts you. Poking along bores and tires you. The result is that you keep thinking about giving up the trip until you actually do. You can become road-weary by being too ambitious as well as lacking enough drive.

The solution is to find your own particular pace and stick to it. That pace probably is a schedule between six and eight weeks on the road.

TRAINING

Without question, you must prepare your muscles for the trip. If you do not train beforehand, you are in pain so much the first four or five days that you may decide to give up the entire project, a decision that can be avoided by getting in shape before you leave.

The extremely simple training schedule in Chapter 2 is a first step. You can supplement this schedule by strengthening your legs, arms, and stomach by knee bends, push-ups, and sit-ups. Lie on your back with your hands supporting your hips and pedal an imaginary bike. This gets your leg muscles attuned to the circular motion of biking. Running in place develops your lungs and heart.

However, no amount of calisthenics can substitute for the reality of riding your bike. For about a month before you leave, ride on increasingly longer one-day trips. Get used to the long hauls uphill. Get the experience of what it means to ride the entire day. Know what it feels like to ride thirty miles one day and then the same distance the following day. If you can indeed ride thirty miles without feeling totally exhausted, feel confident that you are capable of ninety miles a day on your actual trip.

Be kind to yourself by training on a regular schedule. The

effort you put out during the weeks before your D-Day to leave will be rewarded.

Surprisingly, you must de-train once you have made it across country. Just as you gradually develop your muscles to hard work on the road so must you taper off your physical condition if you plan not to ride much on the other end of your trip.

By the time you ride across the North American Continent, you will be in top bicycling condition. Be cautious of this. Once you have reached the other coast, continue to ride your bike five or ten miles every day a while. Do not simply ride into town, avoid your bike for a week, and expect to hop on it again for a quick twenty-five-mile jaunt to the woods. It won't work.

As all professional athletes know, physical conditioning requires constant attention. I had forgotten their rule. When I finished my cross-country trip to Los Angeles from Hancock, New Hampshire, I was in such good shape I almost turned around and biked back home. Instead, I stopped riding completely for more than a week while I visited friends and relatives. Then suddenly I decided to ride about twenty miles to a neighboring town. About five miles later my legs knotted into such agony that I could not turn the pedals. The pain was so sharp that my whole body broke out in perspiration. I became nauseated. All I could do was stop riding and wait out the attack.

Chagrined and dumbfounded, I ended up limping the bike home. I had biked across the nation and now couldn't even ride five miles without buckling. Don't you make the same mistake. Ride a little each day after you finish your trip.

IS A SPECIAL BIKE NEEDED?

No. I rode across country on a good $90 cheapie. It was fanciless and faultfree. I had one flat tire (near Williams, Arizona) and no derailleur, brake, chain wheel, or hub problem. I added the carrier rack, an odometer, toe clips, and air pump. Other than that, the bike was standard and sturdy. I treated it well and it did likewise in return.

You don't need a $350 bike to ride across country. In fact, some of the more expensive bikes are designed specifically for racing, not touring, and unfortunately get in the wrong hands. I've seen some expensive bikes that have turned into wobbling wrecks.

What you do need is a solid, safe, well-built bike that can stand up under your weight and the weight of your cargo. A good $100–$150 bike gets you just about anywhere.

TOGETHER OR ALONE?

People have crossed the country alone, in pairs, and in groups. I know of one man who rode alone from Los Angeles to Boston in twenty-eight days. I know of one woman who traveled alone from Seattle to Pittsburgh. I saw one report of a man and his wife who traveled from Berkeley to Boston on a tandem bicycle. I know two young females who rode together for 2,500 miles after they graduated from college and had adventures galore but no serious mishaps. The style of traveling is up to you.

The advantages of traveling together are several. First, you have each other to prod up the next hill, to complain to about the cars that pass too closely, and to share the weight of the supplies. Groups of bicycles are better seen in traffic, too. For many people it's important to have someone else along to talk with and share the sights. Company on the road also provides immediate help in case one in the party has an accident, doesn't know how to repair a puncture, gets sick, or needs a boost in spirits. Traveling together is often more pleasant.

One of the disadvantages is that you travel only as fast as the slowest one in the group, whether it's a party of two or twenty. If you tend to pedal at ninety revolutions per minute while others go at seventy, you may feel you have to lag below your capacity. On the other hand, if you're the one whose cadence is seventy and the others pedal at ninety, you may feel bad about holding up everyone else. This is no small disadvantage.

Decide early in the game about the compatibility of the

group members. You are together for five or six weeks, a long time constantly to be sharing, or not sharing, each other's idiosyncrasies and pressures. Many friendships are strained by long-distance bike trips. Decide early who cooks and who washes the dishes, who leads and who follows. Be sure to ride with someone you enjoy, someone who shares some of your basic likes and dislikes. Otherwise, you may be at each other's throats over where to camp, what motel to choose, what food to eat, which scenic turnout to stop at, what time to get up, and so forth.

Riding alone eliminates many of these problems. You travel at your own speed. You make your own decisions about where to stop and which route to take. You're on your own completely. On the other hand, you must have strong self-discipline to keep yourself moving forward, since no one is beside you pushing you when you need it. You must be able to fix any bike problem yourself. You must be able to make decisions quickly when they need to be made quickly and slowly when they need to be made slowly. Riding alone you must not panic in dangerous traffic or bad weather. You must forego the pleasure of company but must be open to strangers and not afraid to ask for help when you need it.

In the end, you yourself must decide whether to go alone or with someone. You may even end up going alone because you can't find anyone else who wants to go or has the time. However, base the decision on factors of personality, stamina of both body and spirit, and self-sufficiency. The trip is long and hard. Plan it well in all ways. Choose your partners well even if you are your own partner. If you want to go alone, evaluate yourself realistically.

WEST TO EAST OR EAST TO WEST?

The choice of a starting point for a cross-country trip more than likely is decided by where you are in the first place. If you are in San Francisco, you'll probably start from San Francisco. If you're in Boston, you'll start from there.

However, there is an advantage to starting from the west and traveling east. The wind. The prevailing wind in the

United States, as I've said, flows from west to east. This is especially true during the summer months.

The wind generally tends to flow from the southwest and angles diagonally across the center of the country toward New England. Naturally, there are many local variations in wind direction, but the reliable rule is that wind blows from the west.

A wise biker knows his wind. Other than the friction of the tire, a biker on flat road must overcome virtually no other force except oncoming wind. If the predominant number of days has the wind flowing from west to east, the obvious conclusion is that the better biking direction begins on the West Coast.

Westerners have the advantage. In view of this, some eastern bikers planning a cross-country trip transport their bikes to the West. There they mount their steeds and pedal back home with the prevailing—and pushing—wind at their backs. Do this if you can afford it. If you can't afford it or are among those who like to begin wherever they are and you are on the East Coast, then prepare yourself to fight the wind nearly every day.

I was among the second group. I began in New Hampshire and headed west. During the entire trip I had only three days with the wind at my back, on one of which in central Illinois I rode 151 miles. The other days I had to pedal through headwinds from the five-mile-per-hour breezes up to the thirty-mile-per-hour gales in western Kansas that forced me to first gear on flat road. The next time I travel across country will be from west to east.

Besides the wind, traveling from the west gives you more downhill grade on the central plains that gradually slant toward the Mississippi River. If you have the choice, make no mistake. Go from west to east.

DANGERS

The dangers of riding across country are no more than those encountered on shorter trips. The main one is car and truck traffic. You must constantly guard against drivers who, mysteriously, are threatened by bikers on the road and who get back at you by speeding by too close for safety let alone consideration.

The dangers of the terrain, such as mountain cliffs or desert sandstorms, are real but can be faced confidently by using caution and good sense. However, it's other people that frighten most bikers. Stories of muggers mauling bikers on the open road do circulate and a few of them are authentic. I know of one biker who rode alone into Omaha, Nebraska, only to be faced by two carloads of club-bearing, knife-wielding men who ran him out of town. Apparently, they didn't like his long-hair kind riding through town. I know girls on long trips whose only problem was a man who felt the need to expose himself to them. Other than that, they had no people problem.

On my own trip a couple of people flipped me the one-finger peace sign, honked their horns, and shouted one or two obscenities as they drove by. At no time though was I seriously threatened or mugged. On the contrary, people were most helpful with knowledge of the local routes and places to eat. Many beeped their horns and waved in greeting. The stories I had heard were far more perilous than that. In fact, one friend of mine suggested I take a pistol along to shoot the bums. She was a New Yorker.

Fear is your worst enemy. Believe in the best in people. Yes, you run into a few two-legged rats, but on the whole, people along the highways of the nation are solid, friendly, and good to you. Do be wary but don't let fear alone turn your trip into a worrisome failure.

THE NORTHERN ROUTE

Bikers planning to travel across the top of the country from the Seattle or Portland area must anticipate rugged terrain at the beginning. About 100–150 miles inland from the Pacific Ocean lies the Cascade Mountain Range, an extension of the California Sierra Nevadas. The Cascades extend through Oregon, Washington, and into British Columbia.

They cannot be avoided. They are a high, rugged range with peaks rising as high as 14,409 feet (Mount Rainier in Washington), though you do bike through valleys.

On the eastern side of the Cascades lies the Great Sandy Desert opposite Eugene, Oregon. Then rise the Rocky Mountains, the highest and longest mountain range in North America. The Rockies run through Idaho, Montana, Wyoming, Colorado, and New Mexico as well as into British Columbia and Alberta, Canada. Many peaks tower to 14,000 feet. Bikers cannot avoid the Rockies on the northern route. In addition, the riding time through these high mountains is shortened by the relatively little snow-free time in the passes. Snow flurries sometimes come in many sections of the Rockies in late August.

The Great Plains begin at Great Falls and Billings, Montana. From this point the land slants down to the huge Missouri–Mississippi River Valley about 900–1,000 miles away. The country is relatively flat around Bismarck, North Dakota, and then onward to Minnesota, Wisconsin, and down into the Great Lakes states. Hills do force some hard riding, but they are nothing compared to the mountainous regions in the West.

If your destination is New York City or Philadelphia, you must face the Alleghenies, the Catskills, or the Appalachian Mountains sooner or later. The Appalachias rise no more than 6,900 feet, but they should definitely be a consideration in planning your route.

Bikers do travel the northern route and find some of the scenery breath-taking, especially in the West near Glacier National Park, Yellowstone National Park, or the Badlands. I know of two bikers who left one summer from Seattle and got as far as North Dakota, where one of them fell down and broke his wrist. They had to cancel the rest of the trip. The following summer the same two flew to North Dakota, got on their bikes, and continued the trip to Maine. It was probably one of the longest cross-country trips on record.

If you do choose the northern route, be aware of the rough country you are to face. Prepare yourself both physically and psychologically or you'll be soon defeated.

CENTRAL ROUTE

San Francisco and the surrounding area is the starting point for the central route. Bikers face greater expanses of mountains and deserts from this point. First, the Pacific Coast Mountain Range must be crossed. Then to the northeast is the Sacramento Valley and to the southwest the San Joaquin Valley, where the riding is hilly but not overly strenuous.

Next comes the Sierra Nevada Range, a rugged complex of mountains that in the south end has Mount Whitney at 14,494 feet, the highest peak on the continental United States. If you're heading toward Reno from the central portion of the Sierra Nevadas, you ride through Donner Pass at 7,135 feet.

Once on the downside of the Sierras, you ride into the Great Basin Desert that engulfs Nevada and parts of Utah. This is desert riding at its extreme, with huge valleys, hills, and hot summers. More than likely, you ride through the Great Salt Lake Desert before Salt Lake City, the only major city for hundreds of miles in all directions.

From this point, whether you're passing through Cheyenne, Denver, or Colorado Springs, you must cross the Rocky Mountains. The Rockies are as rugged and high in this area as they are in the north. Keep in mind that Cheyenne is 6,000 feet above sea level (Denver is 5,280 feet above) while Salt Lake City is 4,327 feet. The upgrade plus the rough terrain means plenty of hard work up long, steady climbs.

Cheyenne and Denver lie on the eastern edge of the Rockies. From here the high plateau of the central states slants down eastward from about 6,500 feet to 3,000 feet. You can follow the Platte River to the Missouri River at Omaha, Nebraska, and continue to Des Moines and the Chicago area. Or you can head for Kansas City, St. Louis, and Cincinnati.

All this time you are descending gradually to about 600 feet at the Mississippi River Valley area. As the country narrows to the east, you must face the Appalachias if the major cities on the East Coast are your destination.

The central route offers a wide variety of landscapes, as does the northern route. The mountain ranges that need to be crossed demand hard riding. Be prepared.

SOUTHERN ROUTE

Los Angeles and San Diego are the major lead-off points for the southern route. Relatively small mountains must be crossed before you face the deserts of California, Arizona, and New Mexico and the parched lands of Texas.

The area around Tucson does have mountains, but the major roads generally avoid the steepest part of them. By staying well to the south in Arizona and New Mexico, you can avoid the Rocky Mountains, which end their rugged peaks near Alamogordo, New Mexico. However, around El Paso, Texas, at an elevation of 3,695 feet, the Diablo Plateau forces some hard riding. This plateau touches the Edwards Plateau that Abilene is on. Here begins the drop down the Balcones Escarpment to San Antonio at 650 feet elevation.

If you ride relatively close to the Gulf of Mexico, the land is fairly flat from San Antonio all the way across the bottom of the country. The riding is comparatively easy through the middle of Louisiana, Mississippi, Alabama, Georgia, and up the eastern coast.

Remember that Little Rock, Arkansas, lies at the south point of the Ozark Plateau and Mountains. You may run into the spillover of the Appalachias as you move up through North Carolina and Virginia. For flat land stay below Greensboro, South Carolina, and Atlanta, Georgia.

Except for hundreds of miles of desert, the southern route avoids some of the landscape extremes in other parts of the country. Besides that, fall and winter weather comes much later in the South, which allows bikers to start trips later in the summer or extend their weeks on the road into the later months of the year.

However, biking the southern route takes you through extremely humid country that borders the Gulf of Mexico. Summer months in the South are filled with days of sticky weather and thunderstorms. For some bikers the humidity alone is enough to decide them on another route, especially when that humidity lasts for over a thousand miles of pedaling without an air conditioner.

MY ROUTE

The following is a brief description of my route across-country. I began in Hancock, New Hampshire, but since my suggestion is to travel from west to east, I am reversing my route here. As you notice, I combined parts of the southern with the central route. For my purposes, it was the most direct, the least mountainous, and the most enjoyable.

Here is the route state by state:

Los Angeles to Barstow, California: Take Route 66 (Foothill Boulevard) to San Bernardino where U.S. 66 joins Interstate 15. From San Bernardino (1,080 feet elevation) a steady twenty-five-mile stretch climbs to Cajon Pass at 4,259 feet. After Cajon Pass a drop of about forty-five miles through desert hills and a high sagebrush plateau leads to Barstow.

Today in the desert virtually the only direct highways available to travel from town to town are interstates. Several highway patrol cars passed me when I rode the interstates in the West. None stopped me. Highway patrolmen realize bikers have little choice but to ride the interstates.

In the cities, where the traffic is much thicker, stay off the interstate highways, as the law states. Also, stay off the interstates in the East, where the selection of roads is far larger.

Barstow to Needles, California: This 150-mile stretch of desert has few settlements along the way. Interstate 40, paralleling Route 66, is being constructed. The ride is mostly downhill. About twenty miles west of Needles, the highway goes through South Pass at 2,630 feet before slanting to Needles at 484 feet elevation. This section of the desert is extremely hot in the summer. Needles frequently registers the hottest temperature in the nation.

Needles to Flagstaff, Arizona: Much of Interstate 40 to Kingman has a rough rocky shoulder that must be ridden slowly when it's not safe to ride the main lane. In addition, the old Route 66 in many sections is in drastic need of repairs but probably won't get them since eventually it will be replaced by Interstate 40 from Kingman to Seligman. This section of the route passes through classic desert country until about Ashfork. Then the highway moves up into the beautiful Prescott National Forest mountains to Flagstaff.

Flagstaff to Tucumcari, New Mexico: Route 66 and Interstate 40 coincide all the way on this section. The highway drops down from the pine trees of Flagstaff to the desert floor again, passing through the Petrified National Park, Gallup, and Albuquerque. This section has many settlements fifteen to twenty-five miles apart even though it is still deep desert. Some areas are mountainous, such as the Continental Divide area about twenty miles east of Gallup. The mountain riding here is work but not overly strenuous. Gallup at 6,505 feet drops down to Albuquerque at 4,945 feet. The tail end of the Rockies runs through the area between Albuquerque and Tucumcari.

Tucumcari to Wichita, Kansas: U. S. Highway 54 leads directly from Tucumcari, through slices of Texas and Oklahoma, to the heartland of Kansas and the nation. The drop in elevation from the 4,089 feet of Tucumcari to the 1,290 of Wichita helps make this section relatively easy. Besides that, a strong wind usually comes from the southwest and follows the highway, a boon to bikers who want to make good time and avoid bad legs. The country here is flatland with few obstructions of nature or man. Except for the farms and grazing land, it resembles certain deserts. Western Kansas, pie-plate flat and windy, brings forth images of the flattest member of the Union, but toward the eastern half of the state hills rise gently on the horizon.

Wichita to Jefferson City, Missouri: Almost at the Missouri border, U.S. 54 turns into hilly country. The land turns wooded and the northern edge of the Ozarks makes the riding more difficult. Many small farms line the road, which in many sections need repair or are under construction. U.S. 54 passes directly through the Lake of the Ozarks, a recreational area in beautiful but bumpy country. The hills in this area are not large but they seem endless. Over-all, the highway drops to 628 feet above sea level at Jefferson City on the banks of the Missouri River.

Jefferson City to Springfield, Illinois: U.S. 54 now begins to level out slightly, though the Missouri countryside still remains hilly. Many sections of the highway here have no shoulder, which on a two-lane road makes biking difficult and sometimes dangerous in both truck and car traffic. The farms along here are larger, the clearings deeper. At Louisiana (city) the Mississippi River is crossed, both a major physical and psychological triumph. On the eastern side of the Mississippi, the land levels even more. Springfield, Illinois, at an elevation of 610 feet, is the beginning of a long stretch of flat midwestern country.

Springfield to Logansport, Indiana: U.S. 54 angles northeast across the heart of the Illinois flatland and cornfields. Except for a few minor hilly spots, this area is ideal country for easy biking. U.S. 54 intersects U.S. 24 at Gilman, Illinois. From there the road follows level terrain all the way to Logansport at an elevation of 594 feet.

Logansport to Conneaut, Ohio: U.S. 24 continues to Huntington, Indiana, where it intersects U.S. 224. From there it heads east as it crosses into Ohio and passes through Findlay. The country here is mildly hilly and the highway has many sections without a paved shoulder. U.S. 224 in Ohio is also a heavily used truck route. The country is a well-developed farm area with many small towns built as supply stations for the surrounding households. A cluster of trees on the open horizon is a sign of such a small town in this corn and wheat land.

U.S. 224 runs into U.S. 42 about fifteen miles south of Medina, Ohio. U.S. 42 is in bad repair and should be avoided. At Strongville, State Highway 82 heads east between the massive urban complexes of Cleveland and Akron. It is difficult to avoid traffic anywhere in this area since scores of suburban communities surround both these major cities. However, following 82 to State 91 does eliminate some congestion and, in fact, is quite pleasant in some areas. State 91 goes north on the eastern side of Cleveland until it intersects U.S. 20, which runs parallel with the banks of Lake Erie and on through Conneaut.

Conneaut to Erie, Pennsylvania: U.S. 20 crosses the fifty-mile section of Pennsylvania that touches Lake Erie. On the eastern side of Erie the road is fairly flat.

Erie to Albany, New York: U.S. 20 intersects State 39 at Dunkirk (elevation 600). To avoid the population spillover of Buffalo and Rochester, New York, State 39 at Dunkirk heads east and up through Arcade (elevation 1,480) where it once again connects with U.S. 20 at Avon. This section is quite hilly and calls for some hard riding, though nothing totally exhausting. From Avon, U.S. 20 continues over hilly country to Auburn, where it connects with State 5. By taking State 5 through Syracuse, hooking up with State 92, and then riding back down to U.S. 20 again, the extremely mountainous section of Pompey Center is avoided. U.S. 20 continues straight across New York through beautiful farmland but over high, long, rolling hills that demand good bike legs and endurance until Albany at an elevation of twenty feet.

Albany to Brattleboro, Vermont: New York State Highway 7 heads into Vermont State Highway 9. Biking through the Green Mountains of Vermont is strenuous. The climbs are steep and frequent. For eight miles on the eastern side of Bennington, Vermont, (elevation 682), the highway goes up to over 2,000 feet at Prospect Mountain ski area. Many other mountains get in the way before you reach Brattleboro at 225 feet elevation.

Brattleboro to Hancock, New Hampshire: Once the Connecticut River is crossed at the New Hampshire border, the terrain is milder though still hilly. However, the lakes and forests, creeks and bridges, picturesque towns and lonesome cabins make the biking pleasant.

9

CHOOSING OVERNIGHT SPOTS

The range of overnight accommodations begins with hotel suites and ends with storm drains and cemeteries. The choice depends on your interest and ingots.

What type of sleeping spots you pick depends on your style of traveling. If you like luxury, head for the hotels and motels. If you favor the outdoors with some help from fire-places and a pile of wood nearby, steer toward the campsites and state parks. If you are inclined more toward rugged in-dividualism, stop riding when it gets dark and sleep wherever you are.

Any way is best if it works for you. However, some places offer better situations for bike hikers than others. The little features of a place can spell the difference between security and worry, comfort and unpleasantness, ease and difficulty.

HOTELS AND INNS

Generally, hotels offer the most complete travel services in one building. In most cases, a restaurant or coffee shop is on the same premises as well as a small-item store or counter where you can buy newspapers, tape, travel clocks, note-books, candy, souvenirs, and other low-cost supplies. Room service for meals is standard hotel fare, too. In addition, most hotels are equipped to handle travel questions about routes and accommodations farther up the road. Maps and promotional material about local points of interest are free for the asking.

However, hotel hopping often causes more problems than it solves. If you do try the hotel route, talk with the desk clerk before you register. Find out if the hotel has rooms on the ground floor to which you can easily transport your bike and gear. If rooms are available on the street level, assume you can bring in your bike. Don't ask. If rooms are not available there, find out if the hotel has storage space where you can lock your bike safely overnight. Ask beforehand if a fee is charged for this.

Most hotels are not set up for bikers. Besides that, most hotels are located in the city cores close to business areas and downtown tourist attractions. They cater primarily to a jet-flying, car-driving, cab-jaunting crowd and therefore draw heavy traffic nearby.

The inns in smaller towns, particularly those in New England, are more accommodating to bikers. Normally, an innkeeper tries hard to find a shed or toolroom for your bike overnight since he knows that his inn is usually the only public accommodation in town.

However, the inns are usually comparatively small and, like their bigger hotel cousins, are not set up for bikers. Still, with a little explaining and arranging with the manager, staying at inns can be pleasant and interesting.

Remember that hotels and inns usually charge fairly high rates. You also pay high prices for the convenience of a restaurant on the same premises. If finances are a major consideration in planning a trip, keep in mind that hotel rooms may run $12–$25 for one person.

MOTELS

Motels provide the best spots for bikers who have enough money and are not camping along the way. Motels cost anywhere from $5–$16 for a single room and are usually plentiful enough in a city or town to offer a choice.

Don't steer into the first motel you come to. Think ahead.

Look for the best combination of food, rest, comfort, and ease. You are the power source of your vehicle, so good food and good rest are the octane ratings of your bike.

Some motels are designed better than others. Look for the complexes that are set back from the highway or those with trees and shrubbery between the rooms and the road. You end up with better sleeping conditions if your motel is away from the rumble of trucks that pass on the highway at all hours of the day and night. Better yet, find a motel that is located on a side street off the main road. A room on a side street is far quieter. The extra block out of the way reaps much better rest. A good night's sleep is extremely important. How soundly you sleep largely determines the vitality and energy you have the following morning.

Some motels operate a place to eat on the premises. Pick a motel that is close to a coffee shop or restaurant. Remember that you may not want to get on your bike again in the evening to ride a mile or so to a place to eat.

Some managers offer free coffee and doughnuts in the morning. This extra service can be useful to bikers, especially those who get up at dawn, ride an hour or two, and then eat breakfast. The free coffee and doughnuts in the motel room or office lobby is a small but effective snack to start the riding day with: your eyes are awake and your stomach at work churning out energy to your muscles.

The location of a motel is important in the morning, too. If you're riding through a city, it's better to find a motel on the far side of town. This way you are ready to ride immediately out of the city limits and don't have to edge cautiously through the morning traffic. By basing yourself on the far side of town in the evening, you avoid the incoming rush of cars and trucks the following morning. Since more people come into town than travel out of it in the morning, you find yourself in a relatively traffic-free outgoing lane.

One advantage of motels is that you can easily bring your bike inside the room for safe-keeping, unpacking, and general repair and maintenance. Choose a motel that is built on one level only. Not only are the multiple-story motels inconvenient, but the ground floors are usually priced more expensively than the higher floors.

Always look at a room before you register and pay for it. Some rooms look splendiferous from the exterior but are not worth the price of pudding on the inside. Also, a look at the room tells you that enough space is available for your bike inside.

Assume that it is all right to park your bike inside your room. Never ask permission of the manager. One time, feeling noble, I asked if it would be all right to bring my bike inside the room and was summarily turned down. Tired and sore, I had to look for another motel. Generally, you should find little difficulty this way though.

The motel circuit can be expensive, particularly on long excursions, but it does provide the best sleeping and eating conditions for those who ride hard during the day. A good hot meal and a comfortable bed do wonders to rejuvenate your body and spirit for another hundred miles the next day.

TRUCK DRIVER STOPS

Sometimes large service stations on the outskirts of town have rooms for truck drivers. These rooms and bunks cost as little as $2.00 a night, including a shower.

These roadside stops are designed for the professional truck driver. However, if you find one that has a few empty beds, you often can spend the night at low cost, have a place to wash up, and stay out of the night air. Luxury is not the key word in these places but they do offer an alternative for bikers having trouble finding a place to sleep late at night.

STATE AND NATIONAL PARKS

Bike hikers who camp on route usually choose the state and national parks that line the highways. These parks normally offer good campsites in pleasant surroundings. They are also marked on nearly all road maps for easy planning of all kinds of outings.

Camping out for those who are adventuresome, nature-loving, and poor requires that outdoor gear be included in the bike cargo. Sleeping bag, tent, and cooking utensils are the basics that should be part of any bike camper's gear. This means extra weight to carry on the bike.

However, the added weight provides for enjoyable outings in the woods under starry summer skies. One of the more pleasant experiences in bike camping is to ride into a state or national park and find other bike hikers there, too. A circle of camaraderie soon forms. Bikers greet each other like long-lost friends. Experiences are shared. Travel hints are exchanged. Campfires are lined with bikers telling stories, singing, roasting marshmallows, drinking hot chocolate, beer, or whatever turns them on. The feeling of adventurers sharing the complaints and fun of the open road pervades. Such nights are worth the hard riding during the day.

When you do travel to state and national parks, plan ahead carefully. So you will be prepared, check beforehand to see if charges are collected at the gate. Examine your map to see the distance from the starting point of your day to the park. Know what facilities are available at your particular destination. Some parks do not allow overnight camping. Some don't have cooking facilities. Know what to expect and what not to expect.

Count on the larger parks to be more crowded than the smaller ones. If a park has fishing, swimming, and boating available, know that that park will be crowded with people, boats, children, noise, and claustrophobia. Be prepared.

The smaller parks usually are more pleasant. In most instances, I've found the grounds in a more intimate park far cleaner, the setting more tranquil, and the overnight stay more enjoyable.

Whatever size park you head for, plan to arrive relatively early in the day for two main reasons. First, you have a better chance of picking the campsite you want before other people arrive. It is deflating to arrive in a campground to discover that only the leftover sites remain for occupancy or, worse yet, to discover that none at all are left. No biker likes to be forced to ride on late at night to find another overnight spot when he thought he had one waiting for him.

Secondly, arriving about three hours before sunset gives you ample time to unpack, set up camp, pitch the tent, cart water, gather firewood, wash, cook, and relax. Bike campers usually don't carry lanterns (they weigh too much and are too bulky). Once the sun goes down in the woods, functioning in the dark is not as romantic as it sounds. Better to leave lots of daylight in your schedule so you can relax and enjoy the night around the campfire without having to hassle with washing dishes or pounding tent stakes into dark ground.

Pick a campsite away from the camper-truck and trailer group. Nowadays, these vacationers bring nearly their entire households with them. This includes portable television sets, portable record players, transistor radios, even portable clothes washers, all designed to pollute your ear and irritate your equilibrium.

In general, camp away from bodies of water that attract mosquitoes. Pick sites away from outhouses and water sources. These two conveniences draw people back and forth continually at all hours. Look for sites that are set far back from the highway and as far back as possible from the campground road. On sloping terrain, the sites on high ground are usually better. Look for the sites that have stacks of firewood already chopped. Also, look for the sites under pine trees so that the ground is covered with needles to quilt the hard earth into a soft natural mattress.

You should bring along either a thin plastic sheet or some other lightweight material to cover your bike from the wet air at night. Newspapers work in a pinch. A good idea, too, is to lock your bike at night. Either chain your bike to a tree or tie a rope to the bike and a tent pole. Bikes have been stolen during the late hours when campers are asleep. Take precautions.

AMERICAN YOUTH HOSTELS

The American Youth Hostel is part of the International Youth Hostel Federation. A hostel is an overnight way station for travelers of all ages. The first hostel in the United States was set up in 1934 by Monroe and Isabel Smith in North-field, Massachusetts.

Today, hostels are usually operated by retired couples who like to help people in their pursuit of outdoor living and traveling under their own power. The hostels are primarily designed for low-budget traveling, usually by bicycle, hiking, or hitchhiking. However, in the United States a car, motor-cycle, scooter, bus, plane, or train may be used between hostels.

Many bikers planning long-distance trips join the AYH to take advantage of the low $2.00 overnight fee charged at the hostels. Membership costs $10 for those over eighteen years of age and $5.00 for those under eighteen. The membership passes are valid for one year and are good in forty-seven countries.

On trips all that is needed to stay at the hostels are the passes, a sheet sleeping sack (not a sleeping bag), and knife, fork, spoon, cup, plate, and dishtowel. These items do not weigh much and, except for the sleeping sheet, are included in bike campers' saddlebags anyway.

A hostel can be a farmhouse, school, camp, church, moun-tain lodge, community center, or specifically designed build-ing. Members receive current listings of hostels in all the states and can plan their routes and stays accordingly.

Bikers often find hosteling a good way to meet new people as well as to sleep and prepare their own food in comfortable surroundings at inexpensive rates. Just as in outdoor camp-ing, hosteling has its own feeling of camaraderie. Many times small groups of bikers meet other congenial small groups and join forces for a few days on the road. Bike clubs in different towns pick a hostel, make reservations, and meet for an ex-change of ideas and fun.

Normally, three days is the limit of a stay at one hostel. However, sometimes exceptions can be made with the house-parents. This way a group of bikers can use the hostel as a base from which to take trips through the nearby country-side.

In addition, the American Youth Hostel sponsors many trips. Some are simple, some are elaborate. All the trips are

designed for small groups under a trained leader. Although
hiking trips, station wagon trips, and trips by public transportation are available, cycling tours are the primary type.

These guided bicycling trips are sometimes rather expensive
but are worth it. For example, the Great River Run lasts
thirty-six days and follows the Mississippi River part way
while bicyclists travel through Minnesota, Wisconsin, Iowa,
and Illinois. St. Paul is the start and Chicago the finish. The
biking is somewhat rugged on this particular trip and 60 per
cent of the time is spent camping out. The cost is $305.

The hostel system is well established in Europe. However,
in the United States the hostels are not as widespread. The
majority of hostels here are located in New England, where
fifteen are open to travelers. California, the state with the
largest population in the nation, has only seven. The entire
American system numbers about one hundred hostels.

A new push is currently in progress to develop many more
hostels, but now bikers cannot expect to travel from one hostel
to the next in a day for very far. Only thirty-one states have
at least one hostel available. This disadvantage does not detract from the special affection bikers have for hostels. On
the contrary, it merely prods the development of additional
hostels to keep pace with the burgeoning interest in biking in
this country. In fact, the latest drive by the American Youth
Hostel is to establish hostels only 350 miles apart all across
the country.

As it is now and will be in the future, the American Youth
Hostels offer good facilities and services for bikers of all interests and calibers. A hostel can be a refreshing break for
campers to sleep on a bed, take a shower, and prepare with
ease a good hot meal before hitting the pine-tree circuit
again.

CEMETERIES, JAILS, CHURCHES, OR WHEREVER YOU ARE

Those who find the standard sleeping stations dull and un-
challenging, or find themselves in an emergency situation, can
choose many unlikely but acceptable places to spend the night.
Besides that, the unordinary spots are free.

One young man told me of the time he rode into a small town with none of the usual places for him to camp that night. He was riding across country. He headed for the local cemetery as a place that was quiet, undisturbed, and, to say the least, peaceful. Beside an upright tombstone, he unpacked and crawled inside his sleeping bag. About two hours later two teen-age girls walked through the cemetery and headed his way. Snuggled up in his sleeping bag, he watched them come closer. Then he moaned and groaned ever so quietly and slowly rolled over in his bag. "Well, they ran out of that place like the Kentucky Derby," he said. "Their pigtails were sticking straight out behind them."

Cemeteries in the smaller towns should be on every bike hiker's list of free alternative places to spend the night. Usually, cemeteries are located well off the traveled roads, are thick with grass, have many secluded spots to select from, and are highly unlikely to be invaded by joy riders or muggers. They also offer many cooperative sleeping companions.

Another alternative is the local jail. In many small towns, where the crime rate is low, jails are empty for weeks and months at a time. If you're low on finances, or don't have a place to sleep, go to the police station and explain your situation. Ask to spend the night in the jail. More often than not, your request is granted with a grin and you're home free for another day.

Sometimes you can take your bike inside the cell with you, depending on the lay of the building. If not, a storage room is surely available in all police stations. If you can't rely on a police station to protect your bike, you can't rely on anyplace. In the meantime, you have a relatively comfortable place to sleep besides many stories to tell.

Churches offer another refuge for an orphaned biker on the road. Ask the pastor if you can spend the night on a pew. He may agree or he may suggest you spend the night inside his rectory or home instead. Either way you have a place to stay.

Keep your mind open to every alternative. Never eliminate any possibility simply because you figure that you will be denied permission. Your figuring is an assumption. You don't know for certain until you ask. When you do ask, you may discover that people are far more willing to help you than you anticipated.

Your main objective is to get out of the wet night air. In a tight situation, that means any shelter is feasible. Bikers have slept in hay stacks, tree houses, hotel lobbies, and railroad boxcars. They have spent the night in storm drains, woodsheds, and front porches. Any housing, from a corner in a gas station to a roadside picnic table, a clump of spruce trees, a cave, a backyard patio, an unused truck, or a lean-to you make from cardboard, is an alternative.

Whatever you select, do so with as much imagination about the immediate future as you can muster. Make sure your place for the night is secure. Park on the high side of running water. Camp away from the wheel tracks of any vehicle. Give yourself more than one direction to escape to in a hurry. Spend some time familiarizing yourself with the surroundings. Walk around your place to get to know what is beyond your immediate view. That way you feel comfortable when it gets dark, and you can sleep and dream of bicycles instead of beasts.

10

EMERGENCIES—WHAT TO DO

At one time or another something goes wrong on every trip. The mishap may be small and incidental, like a tire puncture, or it may be catastrophic, like a broken bone.

Accidents happen. Situations beyond your control happen. Bad luck happens. Be prepared.

RULE ONE: DON'T PANIC

In an emergency of any degree, the experience of others tells us that the first rule is to think clearly and not imagine the worst. Whatever happens, don't panic. Keep your wits. Be calm.

Granted, it's difficult to keep calm when all the world about you is whirling around in chaos. Or seems to be. Yet it is this very panic that feeds on itself when it isn't controlled as soon as possible.

Here's one trick that helps bring your senses back in line. When an emergency situation arises and you feel your head jumbled with confusion, simply repeat the word "calm" to yourself slowly a number of times. As silly as it sounds, the effect is amazing. The time it takes to repeat the word over and over again, as well as the meaning of the word itself, relaxes the tightness in your head.

Another trick is to stuff your hands into your pockets or

clasp them tightly behind your back. That way you can't rush to touch your bike or an injured partner. It gives you time to assess the situation before blundering in. The half minute you take to examine an accident is enough to make a sound evaluation of the situation and then, and only then, act. If you act without thinking, that is, in the midst of a spontaneous reaction to the mishap, you are likely to see only part of the problem instead of the whole.

The key word is "calm." This does not mean that you have to act at a possum's pace. On the contrary, acting quickly is often the difference between solving a problem and continuing it. The speed with which you act must be balanced with cool judgment. At the sight of a bent rim, don't panic. At the sound of a breaking bone, keep as calm as possible. At the crack of thunder and lightning, remain composed.

THERE'S ALWAYS ANOTHER WAY

Panic destroys the mental balance that can generate alternatives to remedy unfortunate situations. No matter what, there are always alternatives in any kind of predicament. You must have the presence of mind to sort them out and select the one best suited to you and the problem. If your bike gets a punctured tire on the open road, don't stand around moaning and groaning. Fix it immediately. Get to work. Act. If you can't fix it or don't have a patch, thumb a ride or walk the road. Do something.

If you've fallen off the bike after hitting a pothole, clean any wound with water from your bike jugs or a nearby creek. Cover the wound with a bandage from your first-aid kit. If you have no first-aid kit with you, look for alternatives immediately. Some makeshift bandages can come from part of a T-shirt, underwear, handkerchief, newspapers, tissue paper, plastic bags, gloves, maps, notebooks, dollar bills. Use anything. Use your imagination. The first priority is to protect your wound. Any items you use to bandage it can be replaced. That's better than letting your wound become infected.

If you've lost your hat on a hot day, search for alternatives right away. Make a hat from a newspaper, a handkerchief, an extra T-shirt. Make one from a brown paper bag, from a map, from a string of socks. The point is to limit yourself as little as possible. Brainstorm yourself until you come up with a solution that, even though it may appear outlandish, is still effective. It is this kind of inventiveness on the open road that not only makes bike riding challenging, safe, and adventuresome but fun as well.

RAINSTORMS

Have enough sense to get out of the rain. Some bikers don't. They plod on dangerously through the showers that cloud their vision, ride over slippery roads that can easily spill a bike, and fight the splashes that cars and trucks make passing them. Getting in touch with the rainy elements on a bicycle is not recommended.

At times, however, you get caught irretrievably in the rain. It's not for lack of planning on your part so much as the unpredictability of weather conditions. If you are far from any town or settlement and are in the woods, the easiest way to get out of the rain is to get under a tree. (However, stay away from trees, especially lone trees, in a thunderstorm.) A broadleaf tree is better than a needle leaf. The canopy of a broadleaf is larger and generally thicker. Less rain drips down near the trunk.

If you're caught in the rain in a strange town, several types of shelter are available. The closest gas station with a covering over the pumps is a good choice. Usually, soda pop and light snacks are available here in machines. A service station also provides a covering for your bike, important since rain washes away the lubricant in the movable parts of the bike.

Find a coffee shop or restaurant that has an overhang on the front of the building. This protects your bike from the rain while you can have a bite to eat and wait out the showers. If you can't find such a coffee shop, look instead for one that has a double-door entrance. Many times I have used these foyers to park my bike out of the rain or simply to have it close-by to watch against theft.

Other places to wait in town are the local public library,

grocery stores, department stores, new car dealers, covered picnic areas in parks, train stations, bus depots, auto-repair garages, post offices, school grounds. Most of these places give you something to do and people to talk with or, if you prefer, they can be places to be alone and undisturbed, too.

When you're caught in the rain in open country, you face bigger troubles in finding shelter. Other than farmhouses and barns, the easiest covering is a bridge. A covered bridge, an overpass, or a bridge over a small stream all do the trick. Other possibilities include large culverts under a road, abandoned shacks, unused farm equipment, caves, cliff overhangs. Find anything at all that provides temporary escape.

In continuing downpours you can make a lean-to shelter with your bike as the main prop. Take your ground cover, windbreaker, jacket, or raincoat and angle it down from your bike. Tie it to a tree or weight it down to the ground. Leave enough room to crawl underneath.

Sometimes an extra push through the rain to awaiting shelter is worth the effort and may produce delightful surprises. Once in Illinois, I was caught by a sudden thunderstorm that whipped up all too soon. I was two miles from the small town of Watseka when the rain poured forth. Both sides of the road were lined with cornfields. Up ahead I saw survival in a cluster of trees, the only source of shelter, however vulnerable. I pedaled through the showers while, no question about it, lightning and thunder were cracking the entire planet apart. It was a classic midwestern thunderstorm.

I reached the trees and headed for the closest one to the road. Fortunately, I hit upon a trailer court. The rain, lightning, and thunder overhead continued mercilessly. A big German shepherd ran sheepishly to my tree and together we huddled against impending doom.

Then a woman sent her husband out from the closest trailer to beckon me inside lest I be bolted to heaven. She had spotted me from her kitchen window. I brought my bike to their enclosed patio (the dog dashed to another tree) and waited about an hour for the storm to pass. It didn't.

The three of us struck up a conversation and before long I was invited to a hot lunch. The woman said she had read in the paper about a month before of a young girl on horse-back who got out of the rain by standing under a tree. Lightning struck her dead. She didn't want that to happen to me. After lunch the rain subsided. I thanked the two of them for the good sense they had had that I hadn't, for their beautiful lunch and rainless home, and then, saved by old-fashioned, close-to-the-earth hospitality, rode off down the dry road.

If ever you are caught in a thunderstorm and are near houses, don't wait to be bolted to heaven. Ask to get out of the rain. It's a rare Scrooge who refuses you shelter. You meet friendly, interesting people that way. Besides, it's plain good sense.

INJURIES

A fall from a bicycle can be serious. Treat all injuries, big or small, at once. This is what your first-aid kit is for—to apply some kind of immediate stop-gap remedy until further treatment can be given, if needed.

Always consult the brochure that comes with your kit. No matter how much you think you know or have done for an injury, you might forget some important suggestion. Also, you may find that what the brochure suggests is much easier than what you think should be done.

If you fall from your bike and suffer no more than scraped hands or knees, wash and clean the wounds right away. Use disinfectant or soap if you can. Today, first-aid kits contain moisturized towelettes enclosed in hermetically sealed foil pouches. If your kit does not have these, buy them separately. They are handy for small accidents.

If you fall and suffer a sprained ankle or knee, or break an arm, wrist, or ankle, remain as calm as possible. Call for help or treat yourself. Treat a bad sprain and broken bones the same way. If the broken bone is a compound fracture, that is, if the bone has pierced the skin, do not move the limb until professional help arrives.

A victim with a simple fracture, that is, one in which the broken bone has not pierced the skin, should be placed in a comfortable position to await professional help. In the meantime, prepare a splint made from a board, a metal rod, rolled newspaper, the air pump, even a dozen wheel spokes tied together if necessary. Tie the splint right above the first joint above the injury. Tie the splint again below the joint below the injury. The splint should prevent movement of the injured area. Such movement could cause splintering of the bone and further complications. Get the victim professional help at once.

For simple sprains it is good to apply ice cubes wrapped in cloth, or merely a cold cloth, to the sprain. The cold helps retard the swelling and pain.

Injuries that produce profuse bleeding may result from falls from bicycles. It is possible to hit a pothole at the extreme wrong angle and fly head over heels over the handlebars. Some bikers make sure that the gear levers on the bike are placed below the handlebars so they will not impale themselves in case of such an accident.

If you or anyone else in your party has a severely bleeding injury, the modern recommended first-aid treatment is to apply pressure directly to the wound. Take a clean cloth of any sort and press it on the injury. This stops the flow of blood. Hold the pressure for about five minutes, release it for half a minute, then reapply the pressure.

Never use a tourniquet on a relatively minor wound. A tourniquet should be used only if strong direct pressure cannot stop the bleeding. In other words, a tourniquet should be used only when a hand, arm, or leg is partially or completely severed. In all cases involving wounds with profuse bleeding, professional medical help is necessary.

SHOCK

Bikers should be most aware of shock. This serious physical reaction to a severe injury or emotional upset often goes unnoticed and is left untreated. Too many people do not understand the symptoms of shock nor do they realize its seriousness. If left untreated, shock can lead to unconsciousness, coma, and death.

When involved in a serious accident, look at once for the signs of shock in yourself and in others. These signs are cold, clammy skin, rapid heartbeat, low body temperature, beads of perspiration, paleness from loss of blood, and quick, shallow breathing. Even though perspiration appears, the victim usually feels chilled. He may shiver and feel nauseated. He is suffering from an inadequate supply of blood circulating through his body.

Victims of shock must be kept warm. Cover them with any blankets, jackets, newspapers, plastic sheets, or clothes, anything at all to keep them warm. Also, keep the victim lying down. Do not attempt to move him or allow him to move. These are the only two procedures to take: keep the victim warm, keep the victim lying down. Then call a doctor at once.

OUT OF MONEY

Many bikers underestimate the expense of a trip. As a result, they often find themselves away from home without enough money. Sometimes they are in desperate straits without any money whatsoever.

If you find yourself in a similar situation, analyze where you are and how you can turn your surroundings into cash. It is easier than you might think.

First of all, take a dime for a telephone call. If you don't have even a dime, then ask a storekeeper for one. Tell him that you'll return it after the phone call. With the dime, phone relatives or friends and ask the operator to reverse the charges. You get the dime back. Ask your friend to wire you twenty dollars or whatever to the local Western Union office.

Wiring money works this way. Your friend takes twenty dollars to the Western Union office in his town, gives that office the money, that office telegraphs the office where you are and authorizes them to give you twenty dollars. All you have to do now is repay your friend the twenty dollars.

Ways of making quick small money are limited only by your imagination. I know of two boys who worked their way from one national park to the next by rummaging through trash barrels. They collected all the discarded soda pop bottles and cashed in the deposit on them for enough money to eat and travel.

Try to sell your biking story to the local newspapers. This may buy you a couple of meals. Go to the editor, tell him your money problems, and ask if he would be interested in paying for your story about riding a bike across the state, or whatever you are doing.

Find what personal items you can afford to give up and pawn them for money. Your wristwatch, a cigarette lighter, pocketknife, stone ring, unusual leather belt, anything that can bring money enough for you to survive may be pawned.

Lend your wallet to the local banker. Tell him your predicament. Be honest. Ask him for a ten dollar loan so you can get home, pay him back, and retrieve your wallet.

Offer to stack books in the local public library for a day. Offer to clean up the oil sludge in an auto-repair garage. Offer to sweep out warehouses, back rooms in stores, asphalt playgrounds. Knock on neighborhood doors and offer to cut front lawns, haul trash away, clip the hedges, paint a chair, rake the leaves, repair a fence. Be prepared for some of your offers to be turned down, but keep on trying.

Contact the Salvation Army, the YMCA, a municipal or state social agency that specializes in indigents. Ask the Chamber of Commerce where you can get a temporary job. Go to a college campus and look at the jobs-available bulletin boards. Contact an employment agency for one-day jobs on file.

Abandon no idea, not even the last ditch thought of selling your bike.

NO FOOD

When you're out of food you're out of energy. Without food you can't walk let alone ride a bike. If you find yourself in such a situation, that is, with no money and with no food reserve, try legitimate ways of getting food before you resort to snatching it on the sly.

Normally, people respond generously if you approach

them with courtesy, honestly explain your need, and ask them for help. The first solution should be washing dishes for your food. Go to a coffee shop or small restaurant and ask the manager if you can wash dishes for a hot meal. Tell him why you need to do this. Give him reasons, not just a request. Explanations carry the most persuasive punch.

If you know how to cook, suggest that you can help in the kitchen or behind the grill in exchange for a hamburger steak dinner. If you are in the country, approach a farmhouse and ask to cook your specialty or bake bread in exchange for a meal.

The YMCA, YWCA, Salvation Army, and Rescue Missions in the downtown city cores can provide you with meals, too. In the farm areas or the suburban towns, ask the owner of a place if he will give you a meal for hoeing or harvesting his garden or picking apples in his orchard.

Fortunately, most people are willing to help those who need it. Remembering this, it's better not to wait until before you're starving and deteriorating physically. Ask people. Go up to them. Tell them what you need and tell them what you are willing to do for it. You may be rejected, but certainly not by everyone nor for long.

FREE CLINICS

In recent years the free medical clinics designed to help young people in a casual, familiar, and unpretentious atmosphere have spread from big cities to suburbs. Today, many relatively small towns have free clinics open to anyone who doesn't have the money to pay for medical help.

Bikers in any trouble can find these free clinics in many unlikely towns across the country. They are useful to two-wheeling tourists. Some of the clinics provide emergency housing and food for two or three days until you get settled. Others provide temporary job referral services. All of them give basic medical help in case you need a tetanus shot, penicillin, pain killers for a bad sprain, doctoring for bruises and contusions, and other comparatively minor injuries.

The free clinics can often be found in the telephone

book. Other sources for locating them are passing strangers on the road; local hospitals; school offices; police stations; churches; signs on bulletin boards in food markets or the post office; local newspaper offices. The free clinics are one more alternative that should not be dismissed by any biker needing help, even if it's merely a suggestion on where to sleep for the night.

HITCHING A RIDE WITH A MAIMED BIKE

The best spot to hitch a ride with your bike is at a gas station. Here cars and trucks stop and give you a chance to explain your problem and ask for a ride. This is something you can't do easily on the side of the road.

Pick-up trucks are the best prospect for getting a ride since it's easy to lift the bike onto the bed of the truck. For cars, always carry a couple of stretch ropes to tighten down a trunk door over your bike or strap the bike down on the back bumper.

A relatively major highway intersection with a stop sign or stoplight is good for hitching rides, too. Trucks are more likely to travel here.

Sit down at the counter of a coffee shop and wait for prospective rides. Watch who drives up in a large car or truck and watch in which direction the driver is traveling.

Interstate Commerce Commission regulations prohibit professional truck drivers from picking up hitchhikers. Some truckers do but bikers stand very little chance of getting a ride on these giant haulers. Don't wait for the big trucks to stop.

HOODLUMS

At times bikers are accosted by groups of bored barbarians seeking moments of terror. Usually, this happens when the scalawags pass you in a car. The assault in nearly every case is verbal and nothing else. Shouted obscenities and flipping the one-finger peace sign as they speed by usually fill out the attention span of these mule-headed hoods. What can you expect?

In such cases, the best defense against these annoying attacks is simply to do nothing. Continue riding as you were. Respond with nothing but "steady as you go." Don't give them the two-finger peace sign in return. Don't shout back. Don't challenge them in return in any way, as much as you'd like to. If they gain a spark from you, chances are they will continue their harassment. Once you raise resistance, however slight, they have something to bounce off of and will try to push you further.

In the rare cases when you are forced off the road and stopped by a group of dumb-dumbs, keep alert to all possibilities for defending yourself. Don't attack any group, especially one larger than yours. Keep your fear and panic under control. Bullies like to see fear more than blood.

If their threats are serious, bluff them with any wild story you can think of. Tell them the police are following your route. Tell them you are a government intelligence agent on vacation. You are a trap to bring out hoods on the road for the state police to arrest. You are equipped with a radio transmitter to a group of friends following you in a truck. You carry a deadly weapon. You have a weak heart condition. You are the son or daughter of the state police commissioner. You are a cousin to the district attorney. You are friends of agents in the Central Intelligence Agency. Appeal to powers that they cannot see before them. At the same time, give them a way out. Don't put their pride on trial or they will surely press you further.

If this and all else fails and you are attacked physically by an overwhelming mob, protect your head and face with your arms. Otherwise, counterattack with speed, control, viciousness, and monumental guts. Grab your bike air pump and use it hard. Use your belt as a whip. Keep the goons at a distance. Kick them in the groin. Scream, shout, and roar. Move fast. Throw rocks and beer cans. Fill their eyes with dirt. Run away.

Girls riding alone who are accosted must bluff their way out of tight situations. If that fails and you are physically manhandled, scream bloody murder and don't stop. Claw the apes' faces. Knee them in the groin. Fight the bums with all the noise and strength you can muster to attract help from passing strangers.

For some indecipherable reason, some nonbikers feel threatened by bikers who choose alternative means of travel and fun. Fortunately, in most cases this merely takes the form of insults, jibes, and attempts to make us angry and foolish. Don't succumb to the antics of these one-dimensional nitwits. Ride straight and keep cool. The baby-brains will be bored in a minute or two, as usual.

11

GATHERING INFORMATION

Knowing is better than not knowing. The more relevant information you have in hand about a destination and route the easier and more pleasant is the trip. This is true for a short hop to the local historical monument or for a food-packing excursion to the next state.

Since knowledge is power, bike hikers can save energy by knowing what strenuous routes to avoid, what industrial centers to steer clear of, or which state or national parks to select. Knowing details ahead of time can prevent unplanned and unwanted detours. Facts and figures from people in the know are an important reserve for your trip just as the contents of your saddlebags are. Take as much care in filling your head with information for a bike hike as you do with the choice of food and spare parts for the bike. Preparing for a trip from all angles does not necessarily produce a stupendous outing, but it certainly does stave off unnecessary mistakes and worries.

Preparation of information for a trip should be in proportion to the length and difficulty of the hike. Sometimes a telephone call for a few bits of information suffices for a half-day outing. Other times more elaborate means are necessary for a week-long sojourn. Month-long trips demand even greater in-depth research.

The following is a partial list of sources for bike hikers

to pick and choose from according to the type of trip planned. Some sources are more appropriate than others. However, all of them can help in some way on some trips.

BOOKS

It's Easy to Fix Your Bike by John McFarlane. This is an illustrated repair manual available in spiral binding for easy transport, reference, and use.

North American Bike Atlas compiled by Warren Asa. Has one hundred mapped bike rides in various parts of the country. Available from American Youth Hostels, Inc.

Consumer Guide to Bicycles. This compilation by the editors of *Consumer Reports Magazine* is a well-rounded, authoritative buying guide to the wide range of bicycles on the market. Some of the side features in the book include an excellent chapter on bicycle racing that shows the high spirit and intensity of serious races, chapters on bike maintenance, the history of the bicycle, and accessories you can buy.

Anybody's Bike Book by Tom Cuthbertson. This is a repair manual for multispeed bikes, with emphasis on 10-speeds. Chapters concentrate on the repair and maintenance of brakes, handlebars, stem headset, fork, wheels, and so forth. Drawings illustrate the text.

The Complete Book of Bicycling by Eugene Sloan. This covers a wide range of biking topics, from safety to bike history to bike racing to bike buying and maintenance. It's illustrated with photographs and was one of the first mass-appeal bike books of the current boom in interest in two-wheeling.

The Best of Bicycling edited by Harley M. Leete. This is a collection of seventy-nine articles taken from the leading American bicycle magazine. The articles are short. Many of them deal with touring from a personal viewpoint and are set in such places as Mexico, Vermont, Texas, and Ohio.

Simple Bicycle Repair and Maintenance by Ross R. Olney. All-inclusive, illustrated guide to repair and maintenance, regardless of brand, in easy-to-carry paperback format.

MAGAZINES

Bicycling! began in 1961 as *American Cycling.* The magazine now has a monthly circulation of 20,000 and is the most widely read in the field. It is the first magazine most people think of when they want to subscribe to a bicycling magazine in this country. However, it is not the only one today that is gaining popularity.

Bicycling!
H. M. Leete & Company
256 Sutter Street
San Francisco, California 94108

American Bicyclist and Motorcyclist
National Bicycle Dealers Association
Cycling Press, Inc.
461 Eighth Avenue
New York, New York 10001
    7,500 monthly circulation

Bicycle Journal
Quinn Publications
3339 West Freeway
Fort Worth, Texas 76107
    Tabloid; *6,500 monthly circulation*

Bicycle Spokesman
19 South Bothwell
Palatine, Illinois 60067

The Two Wheel Trip
440 Pacific Avenue
San Francisco, California 94133

Bike World
95 Main Street
Los Altos, California 94022

Le Cycliste
18, Rue du Commandeur
19, Rue Montbrun
Paris 14e, France

ASSOCIATIONS

Many organizations are formally set up to distribute information to bicycle enthusiasts as well as to beginners. They are specifically designed to promote interest in bicycling. Much of this information comes in pamphlets and brochures available upon request. Here are some of the major bicycling-related associations.

> Amateur Bicycle League of America
> 6411 Orchard
> Dearborn, Michigan 48126

Founded in 1920. Has a current membership of 5,000 with 180 state and local clubs. This is the governing body of amateur cycling in the United States, which supervises and controls all amateur bicycle competition. The League sponsors the national championship. It publishes *American Cycling Journal* ten times a year.

> American Cycling Union
> 192 Alexander Street
> Newark, New Jersey 07106

Geared toward people interested in cycling for recreation and competition.

> League of American Wheelmen
> 5118 Foster Avenue
> Chicago, Illinois 60630

Founded in 1880 and has a current membership of 605. Conducts bicycling rodeos, cycle trains, century runs. Represents the interests of biking before local, state, and federal governments. It conducts an insurance program and sponsors the annual Winter Rendezvous in March at Homestead,

Florida. Its publications include a monthly *Bulletin* and a biennial membership list.

Bicycle Institute of America
122 East Forty-second Street
New York, New York 10017

Founded in 1919 and has a current membership of 140 with a staff of five. Includes manufacturers, wholesalers, and retailers of bicycle parts and accessories. It publishes a wide range of free promotional literature, including material on "Bicycle Riding Clubs," "Bike Racing on Campus," "Bike Regulations in the Community," "Bicycle Safety," "Bikeways," "Bike Fun." The institute includes the membership of the Bicycle Manufacturers Association, Bicycle Wholesalers Distributors Association, Cycle Parts and Accessories Association, and the Merchant Member Groups of Bicycle Institute of America.

National Bicycle Dealers Association
29025 Euclid Avenue
Wickliffe, Ohio 44092

Founded in 1946 and has a current membership of 7,000 with a staff of two. Has thirty-two state groups composed of independent retail dealers who sell and service bikes.

Committee for Safe Bicycling
264 Beacon Street
Boston, Massachusetts 02116

Founded in 1956 and has a current membership of twenty-six, including physicians, educators, leaders of youth organizations, policemen, bike dealers, and others interested in promoting health, pleasure, economy, and safety of bicycling. Publishes a brochure on biking.

Bicycle Touring League of America
260 West Twenty-sixth Street
New York, New York 10001

International Bicycle Touring Society
846 Prospect Street
La Jolla, California 92307

American Bicycle League of America
87–66 256th Street
Floral Park, Long Island, New York 11001

U. S. Bicycle Polo Association
c/o Carlos F. Concheso
P.O. Box 565, FDR Station
New York, New York 10022

American Association for Health, Physical Education, and Recreation
1201 Sixteenth Street N.W.
Washington 36, D.C.

BICYCLE MANUFACTURERS

These manufacturers provide you with operating and
maintenance manuals for their bikes, if you own one. Included here are some of the major manufacturers of bicycles.

Schwinn Bicycle Company
1856 North Kostner
Chicago, Illinois 60639

Raleigh Industries of America
1168 Commonwealth Avenue
Boston, Massachusetts 02134

Huffman Manufacturing Company
1120 West Foothill Boulevard
Azusa, California 91720

AMF Wheel Goods
Division of American Machine and Foundry Company
P.O. Box 344
Olney, Illinois 62450

Snyder Manufacturing Company
Little Falls, New York 13365

The Columbia Manufacturing Company
Westfield, Massachusetts 01085

Murray Ohio Manufacturing Company
635 Thompson Lane
Nashville, Tennessee 37204

CATALOGS

Bicycle shops and mail-order houses distribute catalogs of bicycle parts and accessories. Some catalogs cost a dollar or two. Others are free.

Big Wheel Ltd.
340 Holly Street
Denver, Colorado 80220

Cupertino Bike Shop
10080 Randy Lane
Cupertino, California 95014

Wheel Goods Corporation
2737 Hennepin Avenue
Minneapolis, Minnesota 55408

LIBRARIES

Big or small, your local public library can be a wealth of information on biking. Books related to bicycling can be found in the card catalog, usually under the subject heading of "Bicycling." Pertinent magazine articles can be found through *Readers' Guide to Periodical Literature* in the reference section. This is the main index source for magazines. Articles on biking are listed normally under "Bicycling" with specialized articles under such headings as "Bicycle Industry," "Bicycle Polo," and so forth. Refer also to "Cycling." If you need help, ask for it.

The Rand McNally Road Atlas is usually at a local library and can provide a good over-all source to plan routes on long trips. *The National Atlas of the United States of America,* published by the U.S. Department of the Interior, gives a great deal of topological information.

OTHER SOURCES

You can visit, write, or telephone the following places for information that might be useful for a bike hike.

> State police headquarters
> Chambers of Commerce
> Municipal Recreation Departments
> National and state parks
> Bicycle shops
> Sports and outdoor stores